Thomas Aquinas: A Very Short Introduction

VERY SHORT INTRODUCTIONS are for anyone wanting a stimulating and accessible way into a new subject. They are written by experts, and have been translated into more than 45 different languages.

The series began in 1995, and now covers a wide variety of topics in every discipline. The VSI library now contains over 500 volumes—a Very Short Introduction to everything from Psychology and Philosophy of Science to American History and Relativity—and continues to grow in every subject area.

Titles in the series include the following:

Fergus Kerr

THOMAS AQUINAS

A Very Short Introduction

OXFORD
UNIVERSITY PRESS

OXFORD

UNIVERSITY PRESS

Great Clarendon Street, Oxford OX2 6DP

Oxford University Press is a department of the University of Oxford.
It furthers the University's objective of excellence in research, scholarship,
and education by publishing worldwide in

Oxford New York

Auckland Cape Town Dar es Salaam Hong Kong Karachi
Kuala Lumpur Madrid Melbourne Mexico City Nairobi
New Delhi Shanghai Taipei Toronto

With offices in

Argentina Austria Brazil Chile Czech Republic France Greece
Guatemala Hungary Italy Japan Poland Portugal Singapore
South Korea Switzerland Thailand Turkey Ukraine Vietnam

Oxford is a registered trade mark of Oxford University Press
in the UK and in certain other countries

Published in the United States
by Oxford University Press Inc., New York

British Library Cataloguing in Publication Data
Data available

Library of Congress Cataloging in Publication Data
Data available

Typeset by SPI Publisher Services, Pondicherry, India
Printed and bound by
CPI Group (UK) Ltd, Croydon, CR0 4YY

ISBN 978-0-19-955664-9

Contents

Preface

Much of the interest in reading texts from an earlier age lies in working out how familiar and yet how foreign their preoccupations and ways of thinking are. A Christian thinker who died in 1274, and whose works were entirely composed in Latin, is at several removes from most of us these days. Good translations and secondary literature help to make Thomas Aquinas accessible. Recently scholars have begun to insist on the importance of studying his biblical commentaries. He held a post, after all, as *magister in sacra pagina*: professor of sacred Scripture as we might say. The fact of the matter remains, however, even in scholarly circles, that the *Summa Theologiae* is by far the most discussed of his works. Without much compunction, then, I have centred this introduction on the *Summa*, in a necessarily highly selective reading (it runs to over 1,500,000 words); yet highlighting issues and insights that are distinctive of Thomas's approach, if often provocative and sometimes unacceptable to a modern reader. Since he divided the *Summa* in three, I have devoted a chapter to each of these parts: much is left aside, of course, but most of the salient matters are touched on, enough (I hope) to enable the reader to scale an admittedly pretty formidable work.

Thomas belonged to a very different culture and society from ours. His writings are far more deeply embedded in his life, upbringing, and career than a first glance might suggest. I have tried to bring this out in the first two chapters. Then, in the 750 years since his heyday, his thought has given rise to much controversy, beginning even before his death. In the last chapter I offer summary accounts of a handful of these debates – which are by no means all safely concluded.

Footnoting references, signalling quotations, and so on were no part of a 13th-century scholar's duty. He could recycle his own and his predecessors' work without a qualm. He knew nothing of copyright and plagiarism, which are 17th-century inventions. That cannot be my excuse. The authors whom I list in the further reading section will, I hope, forgive my plundering their work in what is, I am sure they will agree, a good cause. Nobody has ever written about Thomas Aquinas who did not want his or her enthusiasm communicated, even at the cost of anonymity, to enable others to discover his work.

Reference system

References in the text are to *Summa Theologiae*: *ST*. It is divided into three parts, the immensely long second of which is divided into two; each part is divided into questions and each question into articles: thus *ST* 1.1.1 refers to the first article in the first question of the first part; *ST* 2/2.4.1 to the first article in the fourth question in the second part of the second part.

List of illustrations

Chapter 1
Life and times

The 13th century, sometimes regarded as the great age of Christendom, with everything in Western Europe controlled by the Roman Catholic Church, was, on the contrary, an age of intellectual crisis with much internal dissent. Western Europe was threatened in the east by a totally alien culture and religion. In 1241, at the battle of Liegnitz, in Silesia, the Mongols, who, unexpectedly, advanced no further west, defeated a combined force of Polish conscripts and Bavarian miners. In 1254, Willem van Ruysbroeck, a Flemish Franciscan missionary sent by King Louis IX of France, reached the court of the Great Khan in Karakorum, the Mongol capital, where he debated with Muslim and Buddhist scholars. Giovanni of Monte Corvino (1247–1328), a Franciscan friar from Naples, translated the Psalms and New Testament into Mongolian and presented the result to Kublai Khan. Twenty years younger, if Giovanni had never met Thomas Aquinas in Naples, then he must have known of him.

Tommaso d'Aquino, as he was known to family and neighbours in the native language of the Roman Campagna, became Thomas Aquinas when he entered the Latin-speaking world of the Catholic Church – as he remains in English usage. According to his first biographer, who was present, Thomas died at the then Cistercian monastery of Fossanova on 7 March 1274, in his 49th year. This puts his date of birth to 1224/5. He was born a few miles further

1. Thomas Aquinas, painted by Justus van Gent, 1476, now in the
Louvre

2. The ruins of the family home at Roccasecca

south, nearer Naples, in the family castle at Roccasecca, now a ruin, in what was the county of Aquino, on the border between the Papal States and the territories ruled by the Holy Roman Emperor Frederick II of the Hohenstaufen dynasty.

Originally from Lombardy, and ultimately of Norman ancestry, which no doubt explains why Thomas was relatively tall and fair, the family had owned Roccasecca since the late 10th century. Thomas's mother Theodora belonged to a Neapolitan family. His father Landolfo was a loyal vassal of Frederick II.

There were at least nine children. Aimo, the eldest son, took part in the expedition to the Holy Land in 1228/9 when Frederick II regained Jerusalem and proclaimed himself King in the Holy Sepulchre Church. On the way home, Aimo was kidnapped by a Christian warlord in Cyprus. Ransomed in 1233 by Pope Gregory IX, he transferred allegiance to the papacy. Rinaldo, nearer Thomas's age, also served on the Emperor's side. He deserted in

1245 when Frederick II was deposed by Pope Innocent IV but was captured and executed for treason. The family regarded Rinaldo as a martyr for the cause of the Church. Marotta, the eldest sister, became a Benedictine nun. One sister died in infancy, struck by lightning, while young Thomas was asleep nearby. Thomas remained close to his sister Theodora. Her husband and father-in-law were implicated in an insurrection against Frederick II. Her father-in-law was caught and executed. Her husband fled to the Papal States but was able to return home after 1268, when Pope Clement IV finally defeated the Hohenstaufen dynasty. In 1272, Thomas was executor of his sister Adelasia's husband's will.

For all his impact on Aquino family life, we have no idea what Thomas thought of Frederick II. His contemporaries knew him as *Stupor mundi*, the 'wonder of the world'. His rule stretched from Sicily to northern Germany. From 1237 until his death in 1250, he was at war with the Popes, first Gregory IX and then Innocent IV, a conflict that grew increasingly bitter, cruel, and treacherous on both sides. Thomas had firsthand experience of the power struggle between Pope and Emperor in which his kinsfolk were deeply and sometimes fatally involved.

Self-effacing as his writing is, Thomas occasionally alludes to his family's military tradition. In connection with the virtue of courage, for example, he unexpectedly cites Vegetius Renatus, the 4th-century AD author of the most studied handbook of Roman military strategy: soldiers may act bravely without the virtue simply because of their training: 'No one fears to do what he is sure he has well learnt' – 'as Vegetius says' (*ST* 2/2.123.1). Perhaps the book was in his father's library at Roccasecca. Elsewhere Thomas writes as if he had dipped into the *Strategemata* of Sextus Julius Frontinus (c. AD 40–193, governor of Britain 75–78), an anthology for the use of military leaders: it would be immoral to deceive the enemy by lying, but one may lawfully use subterfuge in just wars (*ST* 2/2.40.3).

3. Frederick II the Holy Roman Emperor

More broadly, Thomas compares the ascetical practices by which novices are inducted into monastic life with the training to which recruits in the military are subjected. Again, noting that we can get angry irrationally, he remarks that 'a writer may throw down his pen and a rider beat his horse', spontaneously comparing his own studious experience with the outdoor life of his brothers (*ST* 1/2.46.7). Again, he recalls that there is one law for the military and another for merchants: when a knight is deprived of his status he falls under the law relating to peasants or tradesmen – perhaps a hint there of his family's position in the feudal hierarchy (*ST* 1/2.91.6).

On the whole, however, Thomas ignores the wider turmoil in which his family was embroiled. He acknowledges the possibility of establishing a religious order of monks to fight for the Holy Land (*ST* 2/2.188.3), for example, but never considers the morality of the crusades, as we might have expected. (One of the pleasures of reading a medieval author is to discover what it never occurred to him or her to discuss.) Going on crusade was a fact of life, presumably, which raised no theological questions. In the early 1240s, in Paris, Thomas must have been aware of the preparations for the crusade to be led by his austere and pious patron and admirer King Louis IX. Much later, in a seminar, asked whether risking one's wife's chastity by going on crusade without her was justified, Thomas replies that, if she has good reason not to come, and is not willing to be chaste in one's absence, one should not go – which sounds dismayingly like celibate male jocularity.

Unsurprisingly, in connection with waging war, Thomas considers whether soldiering is always a sin (*ST* 2/2.40.1). Early Christians regarded military life, with its commitment to shedding blood on occasion, as unacceptable. By his day, however, soldiering was acceptable. He sets out three conditions for making war lawfully. First, only a prince may initiate military action. Second, there must be a just cause: the enemy must have violated the rights of one's community. Third, the intention of those making war must be right: they must intend to promote good or avoid evil. In effect, going to war to redress an injury must not be likely to do more harm than leaving the injury unaddressed. Thus Thomas endorses the just war ethics that had been standard since Augustine of Hippo (354–430).

Thomas says surprisingly little about the relationship between Church and state, despite intense discussion among canon lawyers at the time. Besides the local conflict in which the family was involved, he must have been aware of the Investiture Controversy, the long-running dispute between the Holy Roman Emperor and the Pope, formally settled in 1122, over who should invest bishops and abbots with their rings and crosiers. In his commentary on the *Sentences* of Peter Lombard, early in his career, he states that the Pope, in virtue of his office, is spiritual head of the Church: every political addition to this essentially spiritual authority is an historical accident. Thomas shows little interest in the political role of the papacy. Again, however, he may have taken it for granted.

Thomas must have been aware of legislation promulgated in 1231 by Frederick II in which blasphemy, games of chance, adultery, prostitution, and the dispensing of love-potions were made punishable offences. His brothers must have joked about it. In 1254, more challengingly, he could not have failed to reflect on the legislation passed by Louis IX providing for the punishment of heretics and those sheltering them but also against taking the holy name in cursing or swearing, engaging in games of chance, gambling, and suchlike, in effect seeking to enforce morality by law. A deeply religious man, Louis IX built the Sainte Chapelle in Paris (c. 1245–8) to house Christ's crown of thorns. He was to die at Tunis, in 1270, on a second crusade to the Holy Land. To back his decision to repress vice by legislation, he appealed to Christian principles. Interestingly, however, while Thomas argued that the purpose of law is to make human beings good (*ST* 1/2.95), he denied that legislation was always the right way to control vice (*ST* 1/2.96). On the contrary, legislation should concern 'only the

7

more grievous vices' – which these are he leaves to the judgement of reason.

There is less evidence in his work of Thomas's early monastic formation, or rather, it is so pervasive as to be almost invisible. In 1230/1, Thomas was sent to school at the nearby Benedictine abbey of Monte Cassino, ten miles east of Roccasecca, at first with his own servant. Founded about 529 by Benedict of Nursia (c. 480–c. 550) the monastery was, and remains, the cradle of Western monasticism. Rebuilt after Allied bombing in 1944, the abbey that Thomas knew was ruined in 1349 by an earthquake. His father made a donation to repair two mills on the abbey estate, the profit from which was to pay for an annual banquet for the monks. He may have hoped that his youngest son would eventually become abbot. For the next seven or eight years, Thomas was immersed in Latin liturgical and biblical-patristic culture, no doubt learning swathes of the Bible by heart – the Vulgate, of course; Thomas never learned Greek, let alone Hebrew. He frequently quotes from the Apocrypha, particularly the Wisdom of Solomon and Ecclesiasticus, the writings received from Hellenistic Judaism, and rejected by the Protestant leadership at the Reformation.

Thomas discusses whether children under the age of puberty (14 for boys, 12 for girls, he thinks) should be admitted as monks or nuns: with permission of their parents they may be accepted as oblates, to be educated (as he himself was); they may not be professed, however, until they have the full use of reason, are able to exercise free will, and are therefore no longer under their fathers' dominion (*ST* 2/2.189.5). If parents are in such need that they cannot be properly supported without the help of their children, then, according to Church law, these children may not become monks or nuns (*ST* 2/2.189.6). To the argument that one should not enter monastic life without first discussing it with friends, Thomas grants, citing Aristotle, that long deliberation and the advice of others are necessary in such life-defining decisions; but he goes on to cite Scripture against bowing to the wishes of one's

4. Monte Cassino, much rebuilt, where Thomas went to school

family, when one has no doubt about one's call from God (*ST* 2/2.189.10). His family did their best to prevent Thomas from joining the Order of Preachers: since he was by then at least 18 years of age, he did not need his father's permission. It is a standard topic in ecclesiastical law: Thomas must have had feelings about the matter, though he remains characteristically dispassionate.

The next phase in his education was dramatic. In March 1239, hostilities between the Holy Roman Emperor and the Pope intensified. Frederick II's troops occupied Monte Cassino. Thomas's father was one of the officers entrusted with guarding prisoners captured at the battle of Cortenuova, some 18 months previously, when, with up to 10,000 Apulian Muslim archers, Frederick II defeated the city states in Lombardy. In the fall of 1239, Landolfo dispatched his son down the road to Naples, to study the liberal arts at the new university, the first founded independently of the Church, by Frederick II, to train officials for the imperial service. At this point his father obviously had no qualms about allowing Thomas to study in a well-known anti-papal environment. Here Thomas would meet the Dominican friars, something the family did not anticipate or welcome.

Thomas presumably studied the seven liberal arts: Aristotle's logic, grammar in classical Latin texts, rhetoric through Cicero, arithmetic, music and harmonic theory, Euclid's geometry, and Ptolemy's astronomy. Less conventionally, he was introduced to Aristotle's natural philosophy, which was still banned in papally founded universities, as at Paris, by a certain Peter of Ireland (c. 1200–60). His commentary on Aristotle's *On Interpretation* seems to have been at hand when Thomas composed his own commentary, back in Naples, about 30 years later.

The college at Naples was only a satellite of the Latin, Jewish, and Muslim cultures that interacted in Frederick II's court in Palermo. Michael Scot (1175–1232?), who learned Arabic at Toledo, settled in Palermo, where he translated Aristotle (from Arabic into

Latin) as well as commentaries on Aristotle by the great Spanish Muslim scholar Ibn Rushd (1126–98), whom the Latins called Averroes. Even if Naples was only an outpost, the significant thing is that, immersed for a decade in traditional monasticism, by the time he was 20 Thomas had also been exposed to the exotic culture that was opening up more freely and fully than ever before: the world of Aristotle, largely unknown in the West, communicated through translation from Arabic, with Islamic commentaries and interpretations. He was never to leave this inheritance behind.

In Naples, about 1242/3, Thomas decided to join the Dominican friars. Founded by the Spaniard Dominic (c. 1172–1221) a quarter of a century earlier, the Order of Preachers originated in the attempt by the Catholic Church to combat the widespread heresy of the Albigensians (see Chapter 3). Like the Franciscans, founded about the same time, Dominican friars – from the Latin *fratres*, 'brothers' – were a novelty, a new kind of monk, living in cities rather than in remote rural estates; clergy yet not under the immediate jurisdiction of the local bishop; thus something of a threat to the ecclesiastical establishment, with a system of governance based on frequent elections and fixed short terms in office. Thomas could not have been attracted by Dominican liturgy and conventual life, however – it did not exist in Naples, as since 1239 Frederick II had allowed only two friars to remain in the city. Thomas was clothed as a novice, probably in April 1244, by Tommaso Agni, who was to die in 1277 as Latin patriarch of Jerusalem – another indication of the spacious world that Thomas inhabited. The Aquino family were horrified. Seemingly at his mother's behest, Thomas was kidnapped by a squad of Frederick II's soldiers, including his brother Rinaldo, and kept prisoner for over a year, probably at Roccasecca, until, seeing his determination (he resisted the prostitute whom they introduced into his apartment), he was allowed to return to the Dominicans.

Why was Thomas drawn to join the Dominican friars? Thomas remained loyal to Monte Cassino in his own way, right to the end:

5. Saint Dominic, founder of the Order of Preachers, by Fra Angelico, 1437–45, in San Marco, Florence

dictated in mid-February 1274 probably in his sister's home at Maenza, his last act as a theologian was to reply to a request by the abbot to explain a passage in Gregory the Great (c. 540–604) about the relationship between divine and human freedom – yet clearly he did not want to spend the rest of his life as a monk at Monte Cassino. The likeliest thing is that he was excited by the whole new intellectual world opened up to him at Naples. Late in life, comparing forms of monastic life with one another, he contended that there is nothing better than an order instituted 'for contemplation and communicating the fruits of contemplation to others by teaching and preaching' (*ST* 2/2.188.7). That sounds like the Dominican Order's ideal.

Thomas was dispatched to Paris. The distance from Naples to Paris is over 1,000 miles. Friars were forbidden from travelling on horseback, though he may not have walked all the way. On this, as on later occasions, he perhaps embarked at Civitavecchia, sailing to Aigues-Mortes then up the Rhône by boat.

In Paris, Thomas attended lectures, notably by his older confrere the Suabian Dominican Albert the Great (d. 1280, over 80 years old), one of the greatest scholars of the Middle Ages. The transcript in his own hand that Thomas made of Albert's lectures on Dionysius the Areopagite survives. He attended Albert's course on Aristotle's *Nicomachean Ethics*. In 1248, he accompanied Albert to Cologne, to set up a new study centre. They arrived in time to witness the laying of the foundation stone of Cologne cathedral. During this period, Thomas must have been ordained priest, though no record survives.

In 1252, Thomas returned to Paris. The theology faculty was riven with strife. The 'secular masters', the diocesan clergy who occupied the principal chairs in theology and law, detested the friars. Being mostly from northern France and Belgium, they resented the advent of these interlopers, parachuted into the faculty for a few years, with allegiances elsewhere and particularly to the papacy. It

6. Albert the Great, Thomas's teacher, 1352, by Tommaso da Modena

did not help that, in 1254, the Sicilian Franciscan Gerard of Borgo San Donnino (c. 1220–76) published a book proclaiming that the third age of the world had begun, implying that the friars were the prophets of this 'new age'. The work was declared heretical, all copies to be burnt. Thomas's allusions are as discreet as usual, but he cannot have been indifferent to this episode. Writing much later, he states that the New Law of the Gospel is already nothing less than 'the grace of the Holy Spirit given inwardly to Christ's faithful', thus ruling out the idea of any further 'dispensation of the Holy Spirit when spiritual men will reign'. This response to the apocalypticism of Joachim of Fiore (c. 1135–1202) is probably aimed at the same ideas as reformulated and exaggerated by Gerard (cf. *ST* 1/2.106).

Thomas left Paris for Naples at the end of 1259, not expecting ever to return. He spent the years from 1261 to 1265 at Orvieto. He was commissioned by Pope Urban IV to compose the liturgy for the Feast of Corpus Christi. The papal court was a centre of scholarly endeavour. Albert the Great was in residence, as well as Giovanni Campano of Novara (1220–96), the mathematician who brought out a new version of Euclid's *Elements*, at Urban's request. Thomas began the *Catena aurea* – the 'golden chain', as it was affectionately known – by far the most read of Thomas's works well into the 16th century: 'Perhaps nearly perfect as a conspectus of Patristic interpretation', as John Henry Newman wrote in 1841, introducing the English translation. 'Other compilations exhibit research, industry, learning; but this, though a mere compilation, evinces a masterly command over the whole subject of Theology.' It is an immense anthology of patristic texts, culled no doubt from the library at Monte Cassino among other places.

In 1265, Thomas was assigned by the Order to establish a study house at Santa Sabina on the Aventine hill, the splendid 5th-century basilica given to Saint Dominic in 1221 and still the headquarters of the Dominican Order. Thomas began to write his greatest work, the *Summa Theologiae*. In July 1268, however, Conradin, Frederick II's grandson, invaded Rome: Santa Sabina was sacked by his troops.

Returning to Paris for a second stint as professor, Thomas found himself in the midst of a crisis provoked by the impact of Aristotle's

7. Cologne cathedral towers, woodcut, 1548

works. For the rest of Thomas's life there would be hostility
between members of the arts faculty (clergy, of course) and many,
perhaps the majority, in the theology faculty, over how to deal with
the new ideas. At some point he decided to integrate Aristotle with
Christian doctrine. In June 1272, his term over, Thomas returned
to Naples, to continue his commentaries on Aristotle, to write up
his lectures on the Epistles of St Paul, and to complete the *Summa
Theologiae*.

The best clue to what he was thinking, when he returned from Paris to Naples in 1272, lies in the letter of condolence that the professors in the arts faculty at Paris sent to the Dominican Order in May 1274: 'For news has come to us which floods us with grief and amazement, bewilders our understanding, transfixes our very vitals, and well-nigh breaks our hearts' – there was no such letter from the theology faculty! They piously asked for Thomas's bones for interment in Paris but also, with more chance of success, for 'some writings of a philosophical nature, begun by him at Paris, left unfinished at his departure, but completed, we have reason to believe, in the place to which he was transferred'. Thomas had promised them translations of the following three works: Simplicius on Aristotle's *De anima*, Proclus on Plato's *Timaeus*, and *De aquarum conductibus et ingeniis erigendis*. This last seems to have been the *Pneumatics*, composed by Hero (or Heron) of Alexandria (fl. AD c. 10–70), a fascinating catalogue of mechanical devices working by air, steam, or water pressure. Simplicius of Cilicia (AD c. 490–c. 560), one of the last pagan Neoplatonists, wrote a good deal on Aristotle. Proclus belonged to the last generation of pagan Neoplatonists: his commentary on the *Timaeus*, one of the few dialogues of Plato available in Thomas's day, was regarded as uniquely valuable. It is striking that the philosophers at Paris expected Thomas to be in a position to procure these works for them; we have no idea what he made of them himself, fascinating as it is to see that he was at least regarded as at home in this intellectual milieu.

Thomas had also promised them 'new writings of his own on logic, such as, when he was about to leave us, we took the liberty of asking him to write'. Thomas's commentary on Aristotle's *Posterior Analytics*, begun in Paris and completed in Naples, was sent to Paris, together with his commentary on the *Peri hermenias*, started in Paris but never finished. There is no evidence that members of the Paris theology faculty ever asked Thomas to write anything for them.

8. Church of the Jacobins, Toulouse, where Thomas's bones are enshrined

On 6 December 1273, however, the Feast of Saint Nicholas, something happened during the celebration of Mass. The result was that he decided to write no more: 'Everything I have written seems to me as straw in comparison with what I have seen.' Presumably he had some kind of mystical experience. According to recent commentators, he perhaps suffered a stroke, likely enough after years of overwork. On the other hand, he was summoned to take part in the forthcoming Council of the Church due to open at Lyons. He started out, fell ill on the way, and stopped off with his kinsfolk. He moved to Fossanova so that he might die in a monastery. He was nevertheless still clear-headed enough, as we have noted, to dictate a letter to the abbot of Monte Cassino. Leaving the *Summa Theologiae* unfinished should be regarded as a decision by a theologian who knew all along that what could be said about God could never be finished, or even stated adequately. Thomas decided to write no more, he was not forced to stop by physical or mental breakdown or by death.

Interred at Fossanova, Thomas's remains were moved in 1369, at Pope Urban V's behest, to Toulouse (not that Thomas was ever there). Since 1974 his bones have been housed in the fine 13th-century Church of the Jacobins, splendidly restored, and now a state-run museum.

Chapter 2
Works

In 25 years of working life, Thomas Aquinas wrote or dictated over eight million words: two million of commentary on the Bible; a million on Aristotle; with the rest divided between records of the disputations at which he presided, many short works, and three large compendia of Christian doctrine.

Biblical commentaries

Taking students through the Bible was Thomas's principal duty. An assistant read out the text and the professor commented, paraphrasing, citing parallels, and so on. Two important commentaries have recently been translated into English. The commentary on the Book of Job (1261–5) focuses on the theology of providence, the suffering of the innocent, the human condition, and divine governance. The commentary on the Gospel of John (1270–2) is increasingly recognized as one of Thomas's greatest works. It is, as yet, only among specialists that these works are much studied: their cut and dried analytical style is so different from the richly imaginative approach of earlier patristic commentary (such as Augustine's), and so different again from the historical reconstructions of modern biblical exegesis, that the general reader is unlikely to make headway.

Disputed questions

Much of Thomas's literary production takes the form of transcripts of disputations in which he participated. Face-to-face argument was an essential part of medieval pedagogy. Disputation as a method assumes there will be conflicting interpretations of biblical and other texts that need to be exposed, considered, and resolved. Thomas proceeds by reformulating a thesis as a question; setting out arguments that run against the thesis, citing authoritative texts (Scripture, Augustine, Dionysius the Areopagite, and suchlike); expounding his preferred answer to the question; and finally returning to the initial objections, admitting them, suitably qualified, or rejecting them, one by one. In *ST* alone, Thomas sets out about 10,000 arguments against the positions that he defends – doing so for the most part dispassionately, making the claims that he will reject as plausible as possible. Of course the method was not intended to reach compromise or supposed consensus. It allowed the disputants to discover the strengths as well as the weaknesses of opposing views; but the aim was to work out the truth by considering and eliminating error, however common or plausible or seemingly supported by authority.

We have three substantial collections of edited disputations. From his first three years of teaching at Paris we have 29 disputed questions, the first of which gives its name to the collection: *De Veritate* – 'on truth'. These are, in effect, the working papers of the young theologian. There are two later collections. *De Potentia*, 'on [divine] power', comprises 10 disputations, all related to questions considered in the first part of *ST* (see Chapter 3), dealing then with the divine nature, the doctrine of creation, and the doctrine of God as Trinity. The collection *De Malo* – 'on evil' – contains 16 questions on sin, the causes of sin, and so on, Thomas's best developed account of these matters.

While good English translations exist, these collections are not the easiest point of entry even for an advanced student.

Philosophical treatises

Thomas produced several important works of pure philosophy. In 1270, back in Paris, in the midst of the crisis over the interpretation of Aristotle, he wrote *On the uniqueness of the intellect against the Averroists*. This highly polemical work concludes as follows:

> If anyone, puffing himself up with bogus knowledge, dares to argue against what I have written, let him not hold forth in corners or in the presence of the lads, who are incapable of judging such a difficult subject, but let him write against this book – if he dares. You will then have to deal not just with me, who am the least in this affair, but also with a crowd of other lovers of truth who know how to resist your errors and remedy your ignorance.

Naming no names, though everyone must have known who they were, Thomas inveighs against professors in the arts faculty who apparently accepted the interpretation of Aristotle's philosophy of the mind that was proposed by the Muslim philosopher Ibn Rushd, whom Thomas denounces as *depravator* and *perversor* of Aristotle's thought. He denounces these colleagues (clergy of course) as 'Averroistas' but does not let his scorn disrupt the rigour of the argument. He takes seriously the idea that, instead of each human being's having a mind, there is some kind of super mind of which our individual minds should be regarded as mere participations. Essentially, his argument is that the Averroist position cannot explain what it means to say 'This man thinks'. Bizarre as it sounds, this resembles 19th-century absolute idealism in the wake of Hegel, according to which the process of history consists of a single mind that, so to speak, experiences itself. For Thomas, anyway, this 'monopsychism', as we might call it, is incompatible with Christian beliefs about the individual soul's accountability under divine judgement, though his principal concern is to clear Aristotle of misinterpretation.

In the same year, Thomas issued *On the eternity of the world, against murmurers*, directed against colleagues in the theology faculty. One of Aristotle's 'errors' was that he believed that the

9. **Ibn Rushd (1126–98), the Muslim philosopher**

world has always existed. Thomas's eminent Franciscan colleague Bonaventure argued that it makes no sense to say that a world that has been created existed from all eternity. Thomas of course believed that the claim that the world had always existed is false: the Bible tells us so. However, contrary to what most theologians of the day believed, he contends that it cannot be proved by reasoning alone that the world did not exist from eternity. For Thomas, the concept of createdness has to do with total and radical dependence on God as first cause of all things – which is a separate issue from the world's having a beginning. He saw nothing incoherent in the idea of a created eternal world. Somewhat provocatively, he claims that Augustine and Anselm, the greatest authorities in the eyes of his colleagues, agreed with him. For that matter, his view of createdness as dependence for existence is not what is commonly understood by creation today, let alone in his day.

Thomas greatly admired the work of the Persian Muslim thinker Ibn Sina (980–1037), Avicenna as he was known in Latin, whose work he had no doubt met at university in Naples. Ibn Sina's learning was legendary. (The most influential of his writings was probably his *Canon of Medicine*, translated from Arabic into Latin in the 12th century and reprinted as late as the 17th.) The short treatise *On Being and Essence*, composed 'for his brothers and companions while he was not yet a master' – before 1256, then, in what was to be a widely read treatise – expounds the metaphysical doctrines held in common by Christians, Jews, and Muslims at the time. Thomas introduces his most characteristic thesis: in creatures there is a real distinction between their being (existence) and essence (nature), whereas in God there can be no such distinction.

Neoplatonic studies

Thomas owed a great deal to the *Corpus Areopagiticum*, writings in Greek by an unknown author who presented himself as Dionysius the Areopagite, converted by Saint Paul (Acts 17:34).

10. Ibn Sina (980–1037), the Muslim philosopher

Scholars now identify him as an early 6th-century monk, probably based in Syria. To add to his near-apostolic authority as Paul's supposed disciple, he was identified with the first bishop of Paris, martyred in the mid-3rd century (on Montmartre), whose remains were housed in the monastery of St-Denis, to the north of Paris, where the master copy of the *Corpus* was kept, from which the translations into Latin were made. Peter Abelard (1079–1142/3) had to leave the monastery for expressing scepticism about the latter identification.

In his inaugural lecture as professor (1256), Thomas shows his debt to Dionysius. The role of theologians, while minor, is nevertheless honourable, in the cascading descent of divine wisdom. Things are disposed by divine providence in such a way that creatures have real effect on one another. To suppose otherwise diminishes God by denying the power to cause things to happen with which rational creatures are endowed. Teachers play a real part in the transmission of knowledge. This is the earliest instance of the general principle according to which creatures are genuinely free to play a real part in running the world and working out their destiny: a principle frequently affirmed by Thomas.

Pseudo-Dionysius, as he has been called since his unmasking by scholars in the 16th century, was indebted to, perhaps taught by, Neoplatonist thinkers, especially Plotinus (c. 205–70) and Proclus (c. 410–65), as well as thoroughly immersed in patristic writers up to Cyril of Alexandria (d. 444). For centuries, in the Greek Orthodox Church even more than in the Latin West, these writings had an authority that was only exceeded by the authority of the Bible itself. Thomas was familiar with all four of the Areopagite's works: *The Divine Names* (the names applying to the divine unity), *The Celestial Hierarchy* (on the angels), *The Ecclesiastical Hierarchy* (on the mediation between the human and the divine realms by the hierarchs of the church and the sacraments), and *The Mystical Theology* (on the union with the One beyond speech and knowledge which this mediation secures).

Dating from before 1250, a copy in Thomas's own hand of Albert the Great's commentary on Dionysius's treatise *On the Divine Names* survives in the Biblioteca Nazionale in Naples. His own commentary, of which there is no English translation, is dated to the years back in Italy (1261–8). Through his study of Dionysius, he was well aware of the Christian Platonism that characterizes the

26

mystical theology of the Eastern Church. Moreover, several of Thomas's key maxims come from Dionysius. For example: 'we cannot know what [God] is but rather what he is not' (*ST* 1.3. Prologue). His account of the angels is permeated with allusions to Dionysius. He is familiar with Dionysius's liturgical vision of the world, which brings the believer into union with the unknown God – even if he is not really enthusiastic about it.

The other Neoplatonic work on which Thomas wrote a commentary was the *Book of Causes*: ascribed to Aristotle (as his 'theology') but identified by Thomas as the work of an Arab philosopher who had borrowed a good deal from Proclus and from Dionysius. An important thesis, which Thomas appeals to in his exposition of the eucharist, and which he knows comes from Proclus, goes as follows: 'Whatever is produced by secondary causes is also and more eminently produced by prior causes, since these are the causes of the secondary causes.' Of this book there is an excellently edited English translation. Though the commentary on the *Book of Causes* comes late in his career, Thomas cites it already in his earliest treatise, *On Being and Essence*.

Commentaries on Aristotle

Much of Thomas's personal study went into 'exposition', as he usually called it, of works by Aristotle. Having embarked on what would become the *Summa Theologiae*, he clearly found Aristotle's *De Anima* very helpful in his own theological account of the soul. Then, if he did not already know from reports, he soon found on his return to Paris in 1268 that influential professors in the arts faculty (clergy, of course), much indebted to the standard Muslim interpretations, particularly those of Ibn Rushd, were teaching Aristotle in ways that threatened Catholic orthodoxy.

Thomas's commentary on Aristotle's *Nicomachean Ethics* was composed in tandem with the analysis of action, virtue, and so on in the *Summa Theologiae*. He was obviously delighted to find that a coherent ethics could be developed independently of Christian beliefs, albeit one that found its fulfilment only in the light of Christian revelation.

Thomas is palpably at home in Aristotle's world: a world that is saturated with purposefulness, a world that is meant to be understood in the sense that it is our nature as rational beings to inquire into the world's order and to come to understand it. Our sense of the intelligibility of the world is not, for Aristotle or for Thomas, a projection of mind onto nature, as it seems to many philosophers and others nowadays. To the contrary, Aristotle's world is a projection of intelligible, teleologically ordered nature onto the human mind.

Good translations exist of the commentaries on Aristotle; it cannot be said that much interesting study of them is available, and in any case there is no scholarly consensus as to whether they are creative or merely pedestrian expositions. Of the 12 studies of Aristotle's works that Thomas undertook, 6 were left unfinished. It is striking that, in what turned out to be his last year, Thomas put so much effort into these commentaries.

Commentary on Lombard's *Sentences*

Of the three major works that Thomas composed, the first was the massive commentary on the *Sentences* of Peter Lombard. Peter Lombard (c. 1095/1100–1161) played a decisive role in the development of theology as a systematic discipline. The *sententiae* are 'opinions' culled from vast reading, organized in four books – God, creation, Christ, the sacraments – and forming the staple of doctrine teaching at Paris and elsewhere right into the 16th century. In Thomas's day and for long afterwards, it was customary for every would-be professor of theology to compose and publish an exposition of Lombard's *Sentences*. More than mere commentary, this should be seen as an original theological work in its own right. Since there is no English translation, and as yet no critical edition of the original Latin, and relatively little discussion in the secondary literature, we shall say no more.

Summa Contra Gentiles

The second major work, entitled (not by him) the *Summa Contra Gentiles*, he seems to have started in Paris in early 1259. A good part of the text survives in autograph manuscript. Much revised, this book reads like an experiment to see how near the ancient Mediterranean world's search for wisdom might come to biblical revelation. The first three of the four books investigate how far the truths of the Christian faith can be expounded on the basis of principles available to non-believers; only in the fourth do the arguments depend on specifically Christian revelation. 'Although the truth of the Christian faith surpasses the capacity of reason', Thomas says at the beginning, 'nevertheless the truth that human reason is naturally endowed to know cannot be opposed to the truth of the Christian faith' – the implication of which is that for us 'to be able to see something of the loftiest realities, however thin and weak the sight may be, is a cause of the greatest joy'.

Summa Theologiae

The third and by far the most famous and most studied work is the *Summa Theologiae*, divided into three parts – on (1) God, one and three, and creator; (2) the journey of the image of God to final union with God; and (3) Christ as the way – to which our next three chapters are devoted. Conventionally they are known as *prima pars* (the First Part), *secunda pars* (Second Part), itself divided in two, and *tertia pars* (Third Part).

The purpose of the *Summa Theologiae*, was, as Thomas says, to set out Christian doctrine in an orderly way, considering how

newcomers to this teaching are greatly hindered by various writings
on the subject, partly because of the swarm of pointless questions,
articles, and arguments, partly because essential information is
given according to the requirements of textual commentary or the
occasions of academic debate, partly because repetition has bred
boredom and muddle in their thinking.

(*ST* 1. Foreword)

While he continued to expound Scripture, and to participate in
disputations, he saw the limitations of these methods of teaching:
line-by-line exposition made grasp of the whole picture difficult,
while energetic debate favoured increasingly subtle refinements,
not always with the focus on central doctrines of the faith. He
sought, not to replace expounding Scripture in class and debating
issues in formal disputations – indeed he carried on doing both,
and he surely expected his students to participate in both – but to
provide a synoptic guide, a bird's-eye view of Christian doctrine,
laid out systematically.

Chapter 3
Summa Theologiae:
First Part

By any reckoning, the *Summa Theologiae* counts among the half dozen great works of Catholic Christian theology. We might as well stick to the Latin title, since there is no satisfactory translation. It is neither a summing up nor a résumé. In the early 12th century it meant handy summaries of doctrine. By the mid-13th century, however, a *summa*, in other disciplines besides theology, had become comprehensive, encyclopaedic, organized – not alphabetically, but according to the author's viewpoint. 'Since the teacher of Catholic truth must teach not only advanced students but also instruct beginners', as Thomas says in the Prologue (*ST* 1), 'we propose in this work to treat of whatever belongs to the Christian religion in such a way as may be consistent with the instruction of beginners.'

How Thomas intended this massive work to be used, or by whom exactly, we don't know. It is sometimes such hard going that his claim to write for 'beginners' has been taken as evidence of his being one more professor with unrealistic expectations. More charitably, he may have been designing a guide for future professors, rather than directly for students. He obviously takes it for granted that his readers have not only completed the standard liberal arts course but are also proficient in biblical studies. Forty years later, in 1308 to be precise, the friars engaged in teaching in his home province were ordered not to use the *Summa* but to stick to expounding the *Sentences* of Peter Lombard.

The origins of the *Summa* are as follows. In 1265, Thomas was commissioned to teach young friars at Santa Sabina in Rome. Perhaps they were an elite. He was authorized to return them to their home priories if they did not perform well. He seems to have begun by expounding Peter Lombard's *Sentences*. A record of the course, identified some years ago in a 13th-century manuscript in Lincoln College, Oxford, and now entitled the *Lectura romana*, covers the nature of holy teaching, the names and attributes of God, the Trinity, and charity. Thomas was evidently dissatisfied. Perhaps, as he reflected on the concept of charity, he suddenly

11. Santa Sabina, the Dominican house in Rome

conceived the plan to rethink the Christian life as a whole in the light of the four cardinal virtues of prudence, temperance, fortitude, and justice, as in Aristotle's *Nicomachean Ethics*, as well as the three divinely given virtues of faith, hope, and charity. Perhaps he saw that much more needed to be said about the moral life, in a way that would lead his students more effectively into the practice of the Christian religion.

He hit on an entirely different scheme, which would result in the *Summa* as we have it. First he would consider God (to which this chapter is devoted); then the movement of the rational creature towards God (Chapter 4); and thirdly (see Chapter 5) he would consider Christ, who 'as man is the way for us to tend towards God' (*ST* 1.2).

The Thomist axiom

'Grace does not destroy nature', as Thomas says (*ST* 1.1.8 *ad* 2), 'but perfects it, which is why natural reason ministers to faith and the natural inclination of the will ministers to charity.' This is the most cited 'Thomist' axiom. He formulates it early in his career as follows: 'the gifts of grace are conferred on nature in such a way that they do not destroy it but rather perfect it'. In fact, the axiom is not exclusively or even particularly characteristic of Thomas. On the contrary, the earliest recorded appearance is to be found in Bonaventure, dated to 1248. The roots of the axiom lie in Greek patristic theology, communicated through Dionysius and well established in the West long before Thomas. Some Christians, including Catholics, regard human reasoning as much too twisted by human sinfulness to be easily fulfilled in Christian faith, just as they are inclined to regard the Christian practice of charity as cutting across the natural desires of human will. To such Christians, the harmonious interaction between faith and reason, charity and natural love, and thus between grace and nature, that is expected by Thomas remains deeply problematic.

33

Theology in the university

The first thesis in the first question of the first part of the *Summa* runs as follows: 'The philosophical disciplines provide such a complete account of everything, including the deity, that any other kind of teaching seems superfluous' (*ST* 1.1.1). The right of Christian theology to count as a university discipline may well require justification today. In an academic environment dominated by the Catholic Church, Thomas could not be serious (we might think) in questioning the need for any teaching about God other than the *disciplinae philosophicae*. By the 'philosophical disciplines' Thomas meant the whole range of the liberal arts, mathematics, astronomy, the natural sciences, metaphysics, law, medicine, and so on. This was all undergoing radical revision, as the newly translated legacy of ancient Greece, mediated largely through Muslim scholarship, was being assimilated. By no means a universally welcomed process, the discovery that things in the natural world, including human beings, could be studied on their own, independently of biblical revelation and Church teaching, threatened traditional Catholic orthodoxy. Some prominent academics in the newly developing arts faculty at Paris seem to have been exhilarated at the prospect. 'All regions of reality', Thomas says, formulating the argument, 'are dealt with in the philosophical disciplines, including the divine – which is why the Philosopher [Aristotle] refers to one part of philosophy as theology or divine science' (*ST* 1.1 objection 2): 'There was no need for any other kind of teaching.'

The new learning seemed to be developing into an alternative to Catholicism, among members of the arts faculty, or so it was suspected by the theologians. Boethius of Dacia (Bo of Denmark: fl. 1275), in his book *On the Highest Good*, defended the possibility of achieving beatitude through love of wisdom. He was assumed to be influenced by Ibn Rushd's version of Aristotle's ideal of the philosophic life as the way to supreme happiness. (He remained a

Christian and eventually became a Dominican friar.) The *Summa Theologiae* might have been composed (though we don't know) to persuade admirers of Aristotle that his *philo-sophia*, 'love of wisdom', was not only quite compatible with Christian assumptions about nature, truth, goodness, and the soul, but actually greatly illuminated them. Thomas did once say that philosophy is a kind of revelation: 'the study of philosophy is in its own right allowable and praiseworthy, because God revealed to the philosophers the truth which they perceive, as the Apostle [Paul] says' (*ST* 2/2.167.1).

On the other hand, in one of his last sermons at the University of Paris, he said this: 'A little old lady (*vetula*) of today knows more about things concerning the faith than all the philosophers of antiquity' – quite a significant remark (we might think) to his assembled colleagues and students at the height of the crisis over the effects on Catholic Christian doctrine of the study of the pagan Aristotle. He said much the same thing in a sermon on the Creed preached probably in Naples in 1273: 'None of the philosophers before the coming of Christ was able, with all his effort on the task, to know as much about God ... as a little old lady knows, after the coming of Christ, through her faith.'

Moreover, Thomas sees two ways of judging the right thing to say or think in matters of Christian doctrine: one acquired by study, the other 'by experiencing the divine', *pati divina*, in a neat phrase quoted from Dionysius the Areopagite (*ST* 1.1.6).

Thomas distinguishes between theology (such as Aristotle's) achieved by the light of natural reason, and 'holy teaching', *sacra doctrina*, based on faith in 'sacred scripture', *sacra scriptura*. Human beings are called to a destiny (he assumes) that transcends our natural capacities to discover:

> We must know what the end is before we direct our intentions and
> actions towards it. Therefore, it is necessary for human salvation

12. Approaching Paris

that some truths which exceed human reason be known through divine revelation.

(ST 1.1.1)

'Holy teaching' is a categorically different kind of exercise from 'the theology, which is part of philosophy' (*ST* 1.1.1). However, Thomas expects these two ways of thinking about God to work in harmony. He does not regard himself as a philosopher; he is a 'teacher of Catholic truth'. But he likes to show how philosophical insights, new and old, are compatible with, and actually supportive of, Christian belief. Moreover, he takes it for granted that theologians make use of the philosophical disciplines 'in order to achieve greater clarity', adding, perhaps unexpectedly, 'as political science uses military science' (*ST* 1.1.5).

Nevertheless, many Christians may have to take on faith truths that can be, and indeed have been, demonstrated by philosophy (*ST* 2/2.2.4):

> First, in order that we may arrive more quickly at knowledge of divine truth. Because the science to whose province it belongs to prove the existence of God is the last of all to offer itself to human study, since it presupposes many other sciences; so that it would not be until late in life that we would arrive at knowledge of God. The second reason is, in order that knowledge of God may be more general. For many are unable to make progress in the study of science, either through dullness of mind, or through having a number of occupations, and temporal needs, or even through laziness in learning, all of whom would be altogether deprived of knowledge of God unless divine things were brought to their knowledge under the guise of faith. The third reason is for the sake of certainty. For human reason is very deficient in things concerning God. A sign of this is that philosophers in their researches, by natural investigation, into human affairs, have fallen into many errors, and have disagreed among themselves. And consequently, in

order that we might have knowledge of God, free of doubt and uncertainty, it was necessary for divine matters to be delivered to us by way of faith; being told us, as it were, by God himself who cannot lie.

According to Thomas, that is to say, natural theology, with theistic proofs, theodicy, and so on, was not a first-year subject. On the contrary, as part of metaphysics, it was for advanced students, after lengthy training in the other branches of knowledge. Secondly, most people are either too stupid or busy or lazy to follow philosophical arguments for God's existence. Thirdly, though there are arguments that he regards as valid, mistakes have crept in, and in any case these arguments are not always compatible with one another.

Existence and nature of God (*ST* 1.2–11)

For Thomas, the world in which we find ourselves doesn't 'just exist', as brute fact, inexplicably, for no reason or by chance. As Josef Pieper, a great exponent of Thomas, once noted, the key to his thought, more or less hidden, lies in the idea of creation – the notion that nothing exists which is not created except the Creator himself.

In the *Summa*, obviously, if we think of the intended readership, Thomas was not attempting to persuade religiously neutral philosophers to agree with him. The famous 'five ways' of demonstrating God's existence, which he happily takes from the philosophers of antiquity, are not an attempt to refute atheism but an effort of faith seeking understanding of itself. Thomas could not have imagined that philosophical arguments were required to justify religious practice. For him, we know ourselves as subject to something higher, we perceive in ourselves defects, which we need a higher power to deal with (*ST* 2/2.85.1). To which higher power we should turn may be a good question, he goes on to say; but 'offering sacrifice is a matter of natural law' – 'all agree on this'. The metaphysical reasoning, independent of divine revelation, by which philosophers in antiquity concluded that there is a God is the same reason by which all human beings know that we must worship – what form, precisely, worship should take has been divinely revealed; but, for Thomas, that worship is required is as naturally rational a belief as that God exists.

The 'five ways' go as follows: (1) motion in the world is explicable only if there is a first unmoved mover; (2) the chain of efficient causes in the world presupposes an uncaused cause; (3) contingent beings must depend on a necessary being; (4) the degrees of reality and goodness in the world must be approximations to a self-standing maximum of reality and goodness; and (5) the empirically obvious teleology of non-conscious agents in the universe entails the existence of an intelligent universal principle. These five arguments, for which Thomas claims no originality, demonstrate, from features of the world, that there is a source and goal of everything that exists.

Thomas is mainly concerned to show that argument is needed. He steers between the view that God's existence is so obvious that no argument is required (*ST* 1.2.1), and the view that no argument is possible because God's existence is purely a matter of faith (*ST* 1.2.2). The existence of God is not self-evident, whatever people thought at the time; nor, on the other hand, does one need to have Christian faith to believe in God's existence.

As they stand in the *Summa*, these arguments yield no more – yet no less – than what the ancient philosophers have in fact demonstrated. In the *Metaphysics* (Book XII) and in the *Physics* (Books VII and VIII), Aristotle laid out at length a proof for the existence of an unmoved mover: something, that is to say, which moves everything else but itself is moved by nothing. As his commentaries show, Thomas was happy to endorse Aristotle's argument. He shows no interest in working out his own original proof. He wants to show that Aristotle's unmoved mover is identical with the God self-revealed in the Christian dispensation. The commentary on Aristotle's *Physics* culminates in these words:

> Thus does the Philosopher in his general consideration of natural things conclude at the first principle of the whole of nature, who is the One above all things, the ever blessed God. Amen.

Thomas probably did not expect his students to familiarize themselves with this, or any other, philosophical argument for the existence of God. The most elaborate, and most readable, set of arguments is to be found in Book 1 of his *Summa Contra Gentiles*, as has been shown in detail by Norman Kretzmann. This is Thomas's most personal attempt to show that the thought of the ancient Greeks and their Muslim commentators was fulfilled in the light of Christian revelation.

For the benefit of the many whom Thomas assumed to be unlikely ever to master the arguments, God has revealed his existence historically to Moses at the burning bush (Exodus 3:14): 'I am who I am' (*ST* 1.2.3).

Long before Thomas came on the scene, the tradition was well established that 'the One who is' is the principal name of God. It designates the eternal, self-sufficient source and goal of all things: *ipsum esse*, 'Being itself' (it needs the capital letter) as Thomas would say, understanding 'Being' not as a noun but as the infinitive of the verb 'to be'.

This interpretation of God's self-revelation was familiar (not that Thomas knew this) to Philo of Alexandria (c. 20 BC–c. AD 50), the greatest thinker of Hellenistic Judaism.

Of course, the expression 'Being' easily evokes images of faceless omnipotence or, for sceptical linguistic philosophers, seems an illegitimate and even ludicrous inflation of an everyday verb. In his commentary on St John's Gospel, dealing with the handful of texts where Jesus is represented as saying 'I am', Thomas assumes that the self-revelation of God to Moses at the burning bush has been fulfilled in Jesus Christ and should be understood Christologically. This is a quite common move among theologians of the day, especially his Franciscan colleague Bonaventure. Thomas, however, does not make much of this, even in the commentary on John. He never makes the connection explicit in the *Summa*.

Divine simpleness

'We do not know what God is but what he is not' (*ST* 1.3 Prologue), Thomas declares, in a formula that, though seldom repeated, remains determinative throughout his thinking. He borrows it from Dionysius. He was presumably aware of the teaching of the Fourth Lateran Council of the Church (1215), always a benchmark for Thomas, according to which God is said to be an 'altogether simple substance or nature', *substantia seu natura simplex omnino*.

God is not a body, like a planet, as many at the time no doubt imagined. (Famously, when the space satellite Sputnik was launched in 1977, Nikita Khrushchev, then leader of the Soviet Union, reportedly crowed that it found no sign of God, only proving that it may be a more common misconception than one might assume.)

Thomas, anyway, has his eye on something much more sophisticated. God is not a substance with accidents, a being with properties – as creatures are. God *is* what he *has* – a much trickier thesis. That is to say: such characteristics as goodness, truth, eternity, and so on are not attributes that qualify God's being. That would make God's essence subject to modification and therefore incomplete. God is not to be envisaged as a substance with accidents, an entity with an array of qualities. God is omniscient, not in virtue of instantiating or exemplifying omniscience – which would imply a real distinction between God's nature and his omniscience. The properties that are attributed in the Bible to God – wisdom, justice, mercy, love, and so on – are not properties in the sense of being added on to, or in principle separable from, God's being. These evidently disparate qualities have to be conceived as identical, in the divine case. We are forced to say this, Thomas thinks, because the alternative would be to make God some kind of creature. To speak of the 'simpleness' of the divine nature is to deny of God any of the distinctions that characterize created things, especially, of course, ourselves. In short, God is not to be conceived anthropomorphically.

God does not belong to any genus – not even to the genus of substance (*ST* 1.3.5). Whatever the temptation to think of God as 'a being', even as 'the supreme being', in a world composed entirely of entities of one kind or another, Thomas's insistence on the 'simpleness' of the divine nature rules this out completely. God should not be envisaged even as 'first in the genus of substance', as 'the prototype' (*ST* 1.3.6). God is not part of the universe, even the dominant part.

God does not enter into composition with other things (*ST* 1.3.8), as we might be tempted to think, indeed as many have thought, according to Thomas: conceiving God as the 'world soul' (*anima mundi*); as the basic form of everything, a view that is 'said to be that of Amaury of Bène and his followers'; and as the 'primordial stuff' (*materia prima*) – 'a really stupid thesis', which Thomas ascribes with a flicker of contempt to David of Dinant.

Amaury (Amalric, d. 1205/7) gave lectures on Aristotle that attracted a large audience. The university condemned his teachings, and in 1209, ten of his followers were burnt to death before the gates of Paris as heretics. His own body was exhumed, burnt, and the ashes scattered. David's writings were condemned in 1210, to be burned 'before Christmas'.

13. Amaury de Bène lecturing in Paris, painted c. 1375–80

The horrifying measures to which the ecclesiastical authorities had recourse reflect the fear that the university was succumbing to an organized attempt to foist a pantheistic religious philosophy on Latin Christendom. When Thomas denounces David of Dinant, he must have remembered that engaging with Aristotle's thought, as he had done since student days at Naples, was, after all, fraught with appalling risks.

God is in everything, 'not as a part or a property but like the agent in an action' (*ST* 1.8). God is not subject to being changed by anything external to himself: nothing is external to God (*ST* 1.9). God is not subject to time or temporal change (*ST* 1.10). Finally, God is unique, singular: otherwise something would be alongside God, constraining him (*ST* 1.11). These are the standard claims in ancient Christian theology, conveniently and compactly set out – by no means uncontested in modern times.

Knowing and naming God (*ST* 1.12–13)

At this point – only at this point, one may remark – Thomas raises the question of how we know anything about God (*ST* 1.12 Prologue). The question is not *whether* human beings can have knowledge of God at all – a question that no modern theologian can avoid: Thomas, by contrast, is interested only in *how*.

His thinking is always end-directed, teleological. His considerations are dominated by whether created beings see God face to face (*ST* 1.12.1), and if so how (*ST* 12.2–5). Even in heaven, knowledge of God – if we mean by that total comprehension – must always elude creatures (*ST* 12.6–10). As for knowing God here and now, no human being can see the divine nature (*ST* 1.12.11). On the other hand, a certain knowledge is available by natural reasoning (*ST* 1.12.12), such as that there is a God, who must be good, eternal, and so on. Rather more may be known of God by the revelation of grace (*ST* 1.12.13), though even this is always knowledge of 'God the Unknown'.

In the following question, Thomas considers whether God may be named by us at all (*ST* 1.13.1); whether we say things about God properly or only metaphorically (*ST* 1.13. 2–3); whether our names for God are synonymous (*ST* 1.13.4); univocal or equivocal (*ST* 1.13.5); if analogical, then is God or the world the analogue (*ST* 1.13.6); whether names for God are tensed (*ST* 1.13.7); whether the word 'God' is a noun or a verb (*ST* 1.13.8); whether the name 'God' is unique (*ST* 1.13.9); whether the name 'the One who is' is the name most proper to God (*ST* 1.13.11); and finally, whether affirmative propositions can be formed about God (*ST* 1.13.12) – which responds to an apophaticism ascribed to Dionysius that goes too far for Thomas.

We might be tempted to follow Rabbi Moses ben Maimon (1135–1204), the exponent of Judaism whom Thomas greatly respected, into maintaining (as Thomas thinks) that when we say that God is good we mean only that God is not evil, or that God is the cause of goodness in things – as if what sounds like an affirmation would really only be another negation (*ST* 1.13.2). Against this radical proposal, Thomas simply declares that this is not what people mean when they speak of God. We speak of God as we know him: since knowledge of God depends on knowledge of something created, one way or another (how else?), we can speak of God only as represented somehow by them: 'Any creature, in so far as it possesses any perfection, represents God and is like God, for God, being simply and universally perfect, has pre-existing in himself the perfections of all his creatures.' Thus, we predicate of God perfections we are familiar with in ourselves – meaning them, however, 'in a higher way than we understand'. Indeed, the perfections we find in creatures (goodness, life, and the like) are attributed more appropriately to God (*ST* 1.13.3), since these realities belong primarily to God and only secondarily to creatures.

Yet, though we never mean anything of God and ourselves in exactly the same sense, it does not follow that what we say is simply equivocal. There is a way we use words, which is neither univocal nor equivocal; we often speak analogically. Thomas does not seem to think there is anything remarkable about this. Using words analogically, he clearly thinks, is a perfectly familiar procedure. This uncontentious analogical use of perfection words in respect of God depends, however, he clearly assumes, without spelling it out very clearly, on the dependence of creatures on God as cause of existence, goodness, truth, and so on.

The most appropriate name for God is 'the One who is' – as John Damascene (c. 655–c. 750) says. Thomas appeals to the authority of the church father whom he takes to be the bearer of the theology of the undivided Church. For the first time, however, Thomas goes further, claiming that the Tetragrammaton is even more appropriate (the four-lettered Hebrew YHWH) – the sacred name which is too holy to pronounce, the name which means 'the

14. Moses Maimonides (1135–1204), the Jewish philosopher

incommunicable and, if we are allowed to speak like this, the singular substance of God' (*ST* 1.13.11). Thomas seems to have picked this up from reading Rabbi Moses.

God's knowledge and will (*ST* 1.14–26)

Thomas never speaks of God as 'a person'. Of course, he uses the word 'person' for the three persons in the divine Trinity. That had long been part of the vocabulary of Latin theology. His word *persona* does not mean an autonomous individual centre of self-consciousness, as we naturally think today. This does not mean, however, that God conceived as 'the One who is' is not 'personal'. As the fifth of the 'five ways' concludes, there is 'some intelligent being by whom all natural things are ordered to an end' – 'this we call God' (*ST* 1.3.3).

True, 'knowledge in God is not a quality or an habitual disposition', as with us; rather, it is 'pure actuality' (*ST* 1.14.1). God's being is identical with God's knowing. By the principle of the simpleness of the divine nature God's knowing is his being: 'if it were other than his substance, it would follow, as Aristotle says, that something other would be the actuation and completion of the divine substance, and we should have the altogether impossible conclusion that the divine substance would stand to it as potency to act' (*ST* 1.14.3). 'In God intellect, and what it understands, and the form by which it understands, and the very act of understanding, are all one and the same' (*ST* 1.14.4).

'Anything with a mind has a will.' For Thomas, however, or anyone of his day, the notion of will does not mean, even in God's case, will to power, domination, command, and suchlike, as we might think. 'We call will a desire or an appetite, though it doesn't only desire what it doesn't have but also loves and takes delight in what it does have.' This is the sense in which will exists in God: God 'eternally possesses the good which delights his will, since it is nothing other than his substance' (*ST* 1.19.1). For Thomas, will, *voluntas*, is aligned conceptually with desire, consent, delighted acquiescence, in short, with love (cf. *ST* 1.20.1).

'Those who say that because nature is deterministic it is not subject to providence, are misled by the fact that human planning cannot change nature but only make use of it' (*ST* 1.22.2). God, however, is the author of nature and that includes the determinism often to be found in the natural order. God, indeed, is 'the cause of our acts of free choice, which means that our prudence is contained within God's providence as a particular cause subject to a universal one'. Thomas plays on the assonance between *prudentia* and *providentia*. The main point he is making here, however, is to establish that God cares for the creatures he has made.

In short, while it might look at first sight that the deity as identified in these first 26 questions of *ST* is Aristotle's First Cause, moving everything but itself unmoved by anything, an eternally blissful fulfilment of all being, Thomas, while delightedly endorsing all this, has been guided also by the concept of God forged in the history of Israel and recorded in Scripture: the God who knows and loves and cares, the God in whose image we humans are made (as Thomas will say). Though he does not think of referring to God as 'a person', or indeed to us as 'persons' – that modern concept had not yet entered the vocabulary – Thomas certainly conceives of God as an agent, with mind and will, and one who cares.

This set of questions culminates in the claim that God is 'bliss', *beatitudo* (*ST* 1.26). What blessedness means, Thomas thinks, rewriting the biblical notion in the light of Christian Platonism, is 'the perfect good of an intellectual nature, whose it is to be aware of its own completeness in the good it possesses, and to whom it is appropriate that what good or evil happens to it it is mistress of its own activities' (*ST* 26.1). At the beginning of the second part of *ST* he will return to this theme: 'There is bliss in God, because his very being is identical with his doing, thereby enjoying no other than himself' (*ST* 1/2.3.2). God's being is his doing: not the doing which is creating the world, but the doing which is the life internal to the Godhead. The doing which is the being that is the divine bliss is precisely not the doing which is bringing the universe about but simply God's being as God is. 'God is bliss, by nature, *Deus est beatitudo per essentiam suam*' (*ST* 1/2.3.1 *ad* 1). 'The divine essence simply is bliss itself' (*ST* 1.94.1).

God as Trinity (*ST* 1.27–43)

The consideration of God, as Thomas stated at the start (*ST* 1.2), falls into three parts: first, that which pertains to the divine essence (*ST* 1.2–26); second, what pertains to the distinction of the divine persons (*ST* 1.27–43); and third, what concerns the procession of creatures from God (*ST* 1.44–119).

For Thomas, as for his contemporaries, human knowledge of God has been established in three waves, so to speak: God as First Cause of everything has been discovered by the wisdom-seekers of the ancient world; God as Lord has been revealed to the people of the Law; and God as the Trinity has been revealed by Jesus Christ. The discovery of God has a history. On the whole, he seems to think, the process has been quite smooth. Of course, the self-revelation of God by Christ to his disciples far surpassed the self-revelation to Moses at the burning bush, and that, in turn, far surpassed the discovery of the beginning and end of all things by the ancient philosophers.

Difficult as it of course is, in the light of modern biblical exegesis, to approach the doctrine of the Trinity by way of assembling the New Testament data, that is the easiest way for us today. That is how Thomas proceeds in the *Summa Contra Gentiles* and in his commentary on St John's Gospel. In the *Summa Theologiae*, however, he begins, not with the role of Father, Son, and Spirit in the history of salvation as recounted in Scripture but with the inner life of the Trinity, the 'immanent Trinity', as modern theologians call it. The focus is on the 'processions' within the Godhead of the Word and the Spirit (*ST* 1.27); the mutual relations these processions imply (*ST* 1.28); and the 'persons' that the relations constitute (*ST* 1.29). The treatment is so abstract and technical that one might be inclined to agree that future professors rather than ordinary students must be the intended readership. Tempting as it is to recommend reversing Thomas's pedagogic order here, and go to the mission of the divine persons (*ST* 1.43), the last question in the sequence, we should resist.

Knowledge of the Trinity is required for two reasons (*ST* 1.32.1). The more important reason is so that we may have the right view of the salvation of humanity, accomplished by the Son who became incarnate and by the gift (or gifts: manuscripts differ) of the Holy Spirit. We might, in other words, fail to do justice to the roles of Christ and/or the Spirit in the dispensation of salvation. Thomas is well aware, as the discussion shows, of Arianism: the ancient heresy, always a temptation, to deny the full divinity of Christ by thinking of him as a creature, with of course a uniquely special role. He shows little sign of interest in so-called binitarianism, the belief that there are only two persons in the Godhead, involving denial of the divinity of the Holy Spirit. He knows about the Filioque ('and the Son'): the phrase widely accepted in the Western Church by 800, asserting that the Holy Spirit proceeds from both Father and Son ('double procession'); and the hostility of the Eastern Church to the doctrine (he thinks they are just wrong).

The other reason is to have a right view of the creation of things:

> For by maintaining that God creates everything through the Word we avoid the error of those who held that God's nature compelled him to create the world. By affirming that there is in God the procession of Love we show that God made creatures not to make up a lack in himself, nor for any reason extrinsic to himself; but out of love of his own goodness.

It may be the less important reason, though in fact Thomas repeatedly attacks the idea that God had to create the world, in particular to complete or complement his own being. Creation and salvation, Thomas wants to show, are grounded in the eternal, immanent activity of God. Thus, what may at first sight look, with the concepts of procession, relation, and person, an extremely abstract approach, entirely detached, turns out, as we get into it, to locate the realities of the world and the history of salvation in the light of the Trinitarian life of God. The historical event of the Word at the Incarnation and of the Spirit at Pentecost are manifestations in the created order of the eternal issuings within the Godhead which the divine persons are.

As Thomas says in a key passage, in which he knowingly makes an option, 'everything is treated in [his version of] sacred teaching under the aspect of God, *sub ratione Dei*, either because it is God himself or because it is ordered to God as beginning and end' (*ST* 1.1.7). It is not just a bird's-eye view of Christian doctrine that Thomas offers, it is literally a God's-eye view of everything, and in particular of the created order. He deals with the internal life of the Godhead first – the 'immanent Trinity' – because he wants us to see the world, and everything creaturely, as created through the Word and loved by the Holy Spirit.

Creation and evil (*ST* 1.44–49)

Thomas Aquinas is not the only Christian thinker who has emphasized the goodness of God and of creation, but it was his main contribution to the most serious crisis in the Catholic Church of his day. The six questions in the *Summa Theologiae* which Thomas devotes to the doctrine of creation culminate in refutations of the idea that evil is a reality (*ST* 1.48) and that there exists one sovereign evil in conflict with God as supreme good (*ST* 1.49). Though he never mentions them, he no doubt had in mind the doctrines of the vast number of dissidents in the Church whom we know as the Albigensians or Cathars. He was alluding to them when he denounced the Manichaean heresy as 'more mistaken than even pagans are' (*ST* 1/2.10.6). The respect for nature that Thomas finds in Aristotle, in other words, is far more congenial, simply because it is compatible with the religion of the Incarnation – which the heresies of the Cathars are not, as he would think.

Thomas presumably knew that the Dominican friars were founded to bring these 'heretics' back to orthodox Catholicism. (The heresy allegedly began in Bulgaria; hence its supporters in France were sometimes called *bougres*.) Albi in southwest France was one of their principal centres. 'Cathars' – a name given to them, not one that they chose – most likely originated from Greek *katharoi*, 'pure ones', first recorded in 1181, referring, no doubt ironically, to certain heretics in Cologne. An elite of devotees vowed to celibacy, to owning no property, to pacifism and vegetarianism, rejected the priesthood and the use of church buildings, and so on, which naturally greatly alarmed ecclesiastical authorities. In 1209, Pope Innocent III proclaimed a crusade that initiated decades of war, devastating Languedoc, with frequent massacres, culminating in 1243 when the Cathar stronghold of Montségur in the Pyrenees was captured – about the time that the 19-year-old Thomas joined the Dominican Order.

Thomas probably never met a Cathar. He must have heard of Moneta of Cremona (c. 1180–1250?), a professor at the University of Bologna, among the first to join the Dominican friars (Dominic died in Moneta's cell in 1221). Dating from about 1241, Moneta's *Summa against the Cathars and Waldenses* must have been familiar to him. In 1252, the Dominican friar Peter of Verona, inquisitor general of northern Italy, was assassinated by a Cathar and canonized by the Pope a year later as a martyr and declared heavenly patron of inquisitors.

The Manichees slip quietly into the *Summa Theologiae*. In connection with the question of the presence of God in everything, Thomas notes that 'In the past there were certain people called Manichees who declared that immaterial and imperishable things

15. Expulsions of Cathars from Carcarsonne, 14th-century manuscript

are subject to God's power, but visible and perishable things to
some contrary power' (*ST* 1.8.3). The crucial move against
Manichaean dualism was to affirm the goodness of God and of
creation.

However, the idea of creation needed a great deal of explanation.
Repeatedly Thomas explains what the doctrine excludes. Indeed,
as he expounds it, the doctrine denies much more than it affirms.

God was not obliged or compelled to create the world – Thomas
insists on this, again and again. 'The first agent acts not in order to

53

16. Montaillou, one of the last strongholds of the Albigensians

get something but to communicate his own completeness, which is his goodness' (*ST* 1.44.4). The world is the result of God's goodness, *bonitas*; 'God's bounty', we might say.

Createdness is simply the relatedness of creatures to the Creator as source of their being: creatures are really related to God in the sense that we are totally dependent on God as the one who keeps us in being. God, of course, for Thomas, is in no way dependent on the world. Creating the world is an ongoing event, so to speak, that God does – but like all God's doings, according to the principle of divine simpleness, creating as God's doing is also God's being (*ST* 1.45.3). The existence of the world, and of humanity, adds nothing to God, in the sense that it makes no difference to God – a radically non-anthropocentric doctrine.

Next comes a highly controversial issue (*ST* 1.46). Thomas assembles ten arguments, mostly from Ibn Sina, Ibn Rushd, and Moses ben Maimon, in favour of the thesis that the created world has existed from all eternity. These arguments employ the notions of possibility, necessity, genesis, space, being set in motion, setting in motion, time, duration, complete and eternal duration. Thomas's first concern is to refute these arguments, thus to show that the world's always existing cannot be demonstratively proved (*ST* 1.46.1) – which does not mean, however, that it is a demonstrable conclusion that the world had a beginning (*ST* 1.46.2). Contrary to what many of his contemporaries thought, he takes 'the same stand here as with regard to the mystery of the Trinity': that the world began is a matter of faith, not something that can be proved. 'It is as well to remember this so that one does not try to prove what cannot be proved and give non-believers grounds for mockery, and for thinking the reasons we give are our reasons for believing.'

Thomas next considers the classical doctrine of Gnostics and Neoplatonists that only one thing can emanate from the One (*ST* 1.47.1). It is a deep question, in the background the kind of mysticism which envisages the ascent to perfection as leaving separateness and variety behind to rejoin the One alone. Consistently with his insistence on the reality of finite things, Thomas does not accept any of this. The diversity of things has been put down to various causes, Thomas recalls. Democritus (d. 361 BC) and the ancient physicists, seeing only the material cause of things, put diversity down to matter alone, treating change as the result of matter in motion. Anaxagoras (d. 428 BC) attributed the distinctiveness and multitude to the concert of an agent with matter, an intelligence which sieved things from the mixture of world-material. And so on. Here, as so often, Thomas is simply quoting Aristotle, he did no firsthand research in support of his learned references.

Thomas then takes on the question of the reality of evil. Arguing with the support of Dionysius, that evil cannot be an existing being or a positive kind of thing but a certain absence of a good (*ST* 1.48.1) – one opposite is known from the other, as light from darkness – so what is evil from the concept of the good. But the good is whatever is desirable, such that every nature desires its own existence and perfection, thus the existence and perfection of anything has the meaning of goodness. It follows that by the word 'evil', *malum*, we mean 'absence of good' – *privatio boni* (*ST* 1.48.5).

The universe of creatures, Thomas goes on to say, is 'better and more complete for including in it some things which can and do sometimes fall from the good without God preventing this' – it befits providence to respect nature not destroy it, as Dionysius says – while Augustine reminds us that God is so powerful as to be able to bring good out of evil:

> Hence many goods would disappear were God to permit no evil. For example, no fire would be kindled were air not spent, the lion would not survive were the ass not killed, and there would be no vindication of justice nor patient endurance to be praised were there no wickedness.

(*ST* 1.48.2).

The doctrine that any evil must always be an absence of good is an implication of the doctrine that everything is created by God and every created thing is intrinsically good. We must not give way to the temptations of Catharist disbelief in the goodness of creation. Thomas is only articulating a long-standing doctrine, which obviously needs a great deal of discussion. Moreover, the give and take within nature is one thing, with the lion killing the ass to survive, and so on – but is anyone's virtue worth the price of another's vice?

The discussion concludes with six arguments in favour of the idea that there is one supreme evil (*ST* 1.49.3). This hydra-headed error is rooted – 'like other strange positions of the ancients' – in their failure to consider the universal cause of the whole of being but only the particular cause of particular effects: 'when they found one thing damaging another such as fire burning down some poor man's house they concluded that the nature of the thing, fire in this instance, was evil' – 'but the goodness of a thing should not be assessed from its reference to another particular thing but on its own worth according to the universal scheme of things wherein each most admirably holds an appointed place'. And here again much more needs to be said.

Angels (*ST* 1.50–64)

The created beings to whom Thomas first devotes attention are the angels (*ST* 1.50–64). Of course, many religions acknowledge the existence of angels ('messengers' in Greek): they appear in the Bible, they play a role in Judaism, Islam, and the Mormon religion as well as in Christianity. In 1215, the Fourth Lateran Council of the Western Church reaffirmed the existence in the universe of a spiritual realm of creatures distinct from human beings, vastly more numerous and incomparably superior in intelligence. Thomas employs the resources of Neoplatonism in a sustained analysis of what is necessarily implied in creaturely forms of life that are by definition bodiless. The Bible speaks of superhuman created beings that are occasionally sent as God's intermediaries with humanity. Thomas's concept of God would in any case make it a reasonable hypothesis that God would create intelligent beings that are not restricted by physicality: 'There must be incorporeal creatures because what God chiefly intended in creation is to produce a goodness consisting in a likeness to himself' (*ST* 1.50.1).

For anyone familiar with recent philosophical debates about personal identity, the discussion of the angels is like a grand thought experiment, an imaginative exploration of a possible world of pure intelligences. Thomas never discusses how many angels could dance on the head of a pin (if any one ever did!), but his considerations would delight the speculatively minded – as, for example, no two angels are the same in kind, each angel is its own unique species (*ST* 1.50.4), an angel can know bodies without sensing them (*ST* 1.55.5; 57.1–2), and so on. According to Karl

Barth, however, the most eminent Protestant theologian of modern times, Thomas may well count as 'the greatest angelogue of all Church history', but his account of the angels is 'a gigantic self-projection of the ego into an objectivity in which it thinks to find in the angel its desired and in the demon its dreaded superior *alter ego*, i.e. itself supremely magnified' (in *Church Dogmatics* III/3, 1961). It would be fun to sort this out!

Human beings (*ST* 1.75–102)

Human nature demands distinct consideration by the theologian, Thomas declares (*ST* 1.75 Prologue), evidently regarding himself as a theologian though in no way reluctant to engage in what he must have known are purely philosophical arguments. Though, characteristically, he leaves it to the reader to see where the discussion is headed, we eventually reach the human being as made to the image of God (*ST* 1.90–102). Everything that he will go on to say, in the Second Part, about happiness, moral psychology, emotions, virtue, sin, law, grace, and so on, will depend on his account of the soul, as will also what he says, in the Third Part, about the Incarnation and the nature of the sacraments.

There is no better translation for the Latin *anima* than the word 'soul' so long as we remember that neither Thomas nor Aristotle (with the word *psyche*) believed in a ghostly entity hidden within the human body. For Thomas, the word 'soul' means the basic principle of life in living creatures (*ST* 1.75.1) Following Aristotle, Thomas argues that a soul, as the primary principle of life, is not itself a body but that which makes a body alive. The soul is not some invisible entity inside the body; but the 'form', or the visibility as we might almost say, of the body. Neither Thomas nor Aristotle sees the soul as connected with inwardness; to the contrary, the soul is naturally public. The soul is how the creature is alive, interacting with things around. This way of existing is marked by sensitivity to the surroundings and readiness to move one way or another. Instead of the venerable conception of the human soul as an exile from a spiritual other world, Thomas favours an Aristotelian notion of the human soul as an aspect of a living organism native to this material world.

In modern philosophy, having a mind and being a person are often regarded in terms of the 'subject', the 'I' as privileged locus of self-consciousness, facing objects out there (including other human beings), apprehended initially as impressions, which we then assemble into intelligible shapes. For Thomas, on the contrary, the objects out there in the world become intelligible as the person's intellectual capacities are realized. Instead of being objects out there, either opposing us blankly or inertly waiting for us to look at them, so to speak, it is the world that has priority, in the sense that objects elicit and configure our cognitive capacities: 'With us, to understand is in a way to be passive' (*ST* 1.79.2). Quoting Aristotle, 'mind is a sort of susceptibility'. Certainly, we have to 'assign on the part of the intellect some power to make things actually intelligible'; but this capacity, which we are inclined to regard as primary or all-important, is, according to Thomas (as to Aristotle before him), secondary. As our cognitive potential is actualized by potentially cognizable objects, we may say that our intellectual capacities actualized *are* the world's intelligibility enacted – or, according to the neat Latin version of Aristotle's axiom: '*intellectus in actu est intellectum in actu*'.

In contrast with philosophical views of the mind/world relationship that presuppose a gap between our minds and things in the world, Thomas develops Aristotle's claim: one comes to know something by the mind's becoming one with the object of thought. The mind's projecting or imposing a structure of intelligibility upon inherently unintelligible objects in the world gives way to a model of how knowledge happens which is participational: the mind assimilates and is assimilated to the object, rather than simply depicting or reflecting it. The structure of elements that constitutes a thought, and the structure of elements that constitutes something that is the case, can be the very same thing. In effect, knowledge is a kind of *assimilation*: the object becoming intelligible *is* one's intelligence being actualized. Knowing is a new way of being on the knower's part; being known is a new way of being on the object known's part. For Thomas, meaning is the mind's perfection, the coming to fulfilment of the human being's intellectual powers; simultaneously, it is the world's intelligibility being realized.

Philosophers are unlikely to be persuaded merely by Thomas's Aristotelian axiom: 'soul is in a certain way everything'. His confidence that things really are as they show themselves, that there is no veil between the world and our minds, matches his belief in the world's belonging to God. What shows itself is the case. There is a certain fittingness of world to mind, of entity to intellect, *convenientia entis ad intellectum*. Our experience of things is not a confrontation with something utterly alien, but a way of being the world to which we naturally belong. We are inclined to begin with the mind, asking how our mental acts ever hook up with the world outside. In contrast, Thomas begins with the world, with what is the case, external objects which evoke intellectual activity on our part, and thus actualize the capacities with which we are endowed.

We assume that the objects of our knowledge remain totally unaffected. To be known, for an object unaware of it, is as if nothing had happened. On Thomas's view, articulating as it does the doctrine of creation in terms of the metaphysics of participation, the object, in being known by the subject, is brought into the light and to that extent its nature and destiny are fulfilled. It is easy to see how our minds are affected, by absorbing what comes to view in the world. But for Thomas it makes sense to hold that, even if there were no human minds, things would still be 'true' – in relation, that is, to God's mind. He does not look at the world and see it as just what is the case, in itself; rather, he sees the world, and things in it, as destined to a certain fulfilment, with appointed ends, modes, and opportunities. It is not too much to say that, for Thomas, as for Aristotle, the forms embodied in the natural world attain an altogether higher level of reality in our minds – because, as already for Aristotle, the world constitutes an intelligible whole in virtue of its dependence on the divine mind.

When he comes to consider the notion of conscience, it is no surprise to find, Thomas denies that it is, properly speaking, a faculty, as we tend to think today; rather, conscience is 'applying our knowledge to what we do' (*ST* 1.79.13). Conscience is not an inner voice addressed to the individual but an exercise of practical reason, in principle open to discussion. Thomas even thinks of conscience, etymologically, as *con-scientia*: 'knowledge with', as something that is shareable, not something essentially 'private'.

The whole series of questions on the nature of the human soul (*ST* 1.75–89) culminates by considering the cognitive situation, so to speak, of the 'separated soul', *anima separata*. For Thomas, as we should expect by now, it was for the human soul's good that it was united to a body and that it understands by turning to sensible images (*ST* 1.89.1) – there is nothing regrettable about our being embodied and our minds being dependent on the visible, sense-perceptible world. Once again, Thomas takes the opportunity to confirm his repudiation of neo-Gnostic suspicions of this world and the body.

On the other hand, 'it is possible for the soul to exist apart from the body, and also to understand in another way' (*ST* 1.89.1). What is to be said about the minds of the saints in heaven, engaged in face-to-face vision of God? Thomas denies that they understand by innate ideas (*species*) or by ideas retained from their previous condition – rather, the souls in heaven 'understand by means of participated ideas resulting from the influence of the divine light, shared by the soul as by other separate substances (the angels), though in a lesser degree'. In short, as soon as we are dead 'the soul turns at once to what is above it, nor is this way of knowledge unnatural, for God is the author of the influx both of the light of grace and of the light of nature' (*ST* 1.89.1).

As the First Part moves towards its end, two salient themes should be mentioned: the moral agent as made in the divine image and the theory of double agency.

The Book of Genesis 1:26 is of course the starting point. There is a sense in which the whole world is after God's image, but, Thomas insists, only intelligent creatures are properly speaking made to God's image (*ST* 1.93.2). It is in virtue of our intellectual nature that we are said to be in God's image (*ST* 1.93.6). The divine image is found in everyone, including women (it evidently needed to be said) (*ST* 1.93.4). The image of God is realized in us, in its fullness in people who are saintly, in our actually knowing and loving (93.7). We might say that, for Thomas, a human being images God dynamically, in the event of worshipping.

Divine government (*ST* 1.103–190)

Largely from Dionysius Thomas has a strong sense of the Platonic tradition of the 'self-diffusiveness of the Good': every being tends, by the inner dynamic of its act of existing, to overflow into action, action that is simultaneously self-manifestation and self-communication. This natural tendency to self-giving and thus to interacting with others is a revelation of the natural 'generosity' that characterizes the creative act of being itself. In other words, causing is always on analogy with the individual's interacting in an endless number of ways with things and bringing things about. Thomas was familiar, through his reading of Aristotle, with the world picture, attributed to the 5th-century BC philosopher Democritus, according to which our world and the kinds of beings in it arise from the collision of atoms whirling arbitrarily in a void. For Thomas, as for Aristotle, the world is conceived teleologically:

things fit together, in a multiplicity of ways, forming a kind of hierarchic community.

Whether cooperation is necessarily founded on competition, even in conflict, is the question. The three arguments that Thomas considers go as follows: (1) if God is active in everything that acts, his action surely suffices – it would be redundant for any created cause to act at all ('occasionalism'); (2) if an action of a creature issues from God working in the creature, it cannot at the same time issue from the creature (one action cannot issue simultaneously from two agents); and (3) God may be said to bestow on creatures the power to act but is not further involved in their acting (a form of deism).

This takes us right to the heart of Thomas's theology. 'Lord, thou hast wrought all our works in us', he often quotes (Isaiah 26.12) – which he serenely takes (e.g. at *ST* 1.105.5) as *excluding* all competitiveness between divine and human agency. On the other hand, when he speaks of 'cooperation' between creatures and God, he frequently alludes to the picture of two rival agents on a level playing field, ruling it out – yet seeming to recognize that this is a strong temptation. For Thomas, it is the mark of God's freedom, and ours, that God 'causes' everything that we humans do in such a way that we 'cause' it too. But Thomas is well aware how difficult it is to keep hold of this thought. If the action by which an effect is produced proceeds from a human agent, we are tempted to think, it surely does not need to be attributed to God as well. When a thing can be done adequately by one agent, it is superfluous to posit another: either God or the human agent does whatever it is. If God produces the entire natural effect, surely nothing is left for the human agent to do. Such are the bewitching thoughts Thomas seeks to dissolve. As he quite flatly asserts, there is nothing to stop us from thinking that the same effect is produced by a lower agent and by God – by both, of course, in different ways. Easy to say, one may object; not so easy to follow through.

Yet, for Thomas, it is always by divine power that the human agent produces his or her own proper effect: that is the doctrine of creation. It is not superfluous, even if in principle God can by himself produce all natural effects, for them to be produced by us as causes. Nor is this a result of the inadequacy of divine power, as one might be tempted to think. On the contrary: it is the gift of divine goodness (*bonitas* = bounty). According to the doctrine of creation, God wills to communicate his likeness to things not only so that they might exist but also that they too might *cause* in their own way.

Our reading has been very selective. We don't know what Thomas hoped his students would take away from the First Part. The salient points may be summarized as follows.

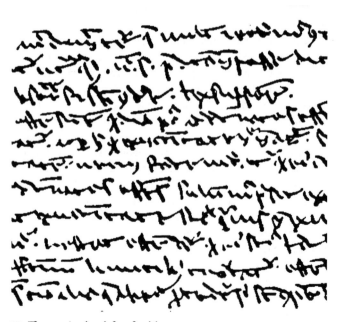

17. Thomas Aquinas's handwriting

Much is truly said about God in philosophy but, according to Christian revelation, human desire for happiness can be fulfilled only in union with God; there is no disharmony between philosophy and theology, to the contrary, faith fulfils reason, the legacy of ancient Greece can and should for the most part be welcomed into Christian theology. God's existence is neither self-evident nor purely a matter of faith. God is 'the One who is', as revealed to Moses at the burning bush. God is not a being of any kind. God is under no compulsion to create; the world is sheer gift. Creatures such as human beings are endowed with reason and free will, made in the divine image, are genuinely agents of their own moral achievements – and in no sense in competition with God.

This takes us to the Second Part of *ST*: 'the movement of the rational creatures to God', the moral life, as we may say, as a journey into sharing divine bliss.

Chapter 4
Summa Theologiae:
Second Part

Thomas Aquinas had composed nothing quite like the Second Part of the *Summa Theologiae*. Unwilling to leave his students with only the confessors' handbooks of the day, he wanted these future pastors to have their 'practical theology' inserted between the two mysteries of faith: God as Creator (in the First Part) and Christ as the way to ultimate beatitude (in the Third Part). Moreover, instead of a checklist of sins, determined by conformity with the Ten Commandments, he drew copiously on Aristotle's *Nicomachean Ethics* to develop an ethics based not on obedience to commandments but aimed at formation of character, envisaging formation as the actualization of the individual potential, the fulfilment of the believer's natural desire for the good under the inspiration of divine grace and (of course) in obedience to divine law.

Invoking the authority of John Damascene again, he reaffirms that the human creature is said (in the Bible he means) to be made to God's image, in the sense (as the tradition maintained) of being 'an intelligent being endowed with free-will and self-movement'. That is to say, 'having treated of the exemplar, namely God, and of what has come forth from the power of God in accordance with his will, it remains for us to treat of his image, inasmuch as the human creature too is principle of his actions as having free-will and control of his actions' (*ST* 1/2 Prologue). And then, since 'the end is the principle in human operations', as Aristotle says, meaning that the goal is what instigates human activity, and the goal is of course the good, this study of the formation of the moral agent will unroll under the heading of human desire for happiness as conceived principally by Aristotle, which meshes harmoniously with creaturely desire for participation in divine bliss, as in Christian tradition, represented by Augustine and Dionysius the Areopagite.

Purpose and happiness (*ST* 1/2.1–5)

The first part of the Second Part sets out the general structure of the moral life; the second part of the Second Part, much longer, offers a systematic account of as many of the virtues and corresponding vices as Thomas can encompass. Ironically, within 20 years of his death, summaries of his treatment of the virtues and vices were in circulation, which suggests that his intended readers were quite content with checklists, more of sins than of virtues, while happily ignoring the analysis of action, intention, choice, and so on, which Thomas regarded as essential for would-be spiritual guides and pastors.

The ultimate goal of human life will always transcend any natural good or set of goods (*ST* 1/2.1–5). Nothing but God, as known and loved in the promised beatific vision, can fully satisfy the human desire for knowledge of the truth and union with the good. None of the goods of this life will ever satisfy us, desirable and worthwhile as they of course are (no concessions to Catharist contempt of the material world). This is one of Thomas's fundamental convictions. If we required argument to convince us that human beings desire to be happy, Thomas would have been quite baffled – he took that for granted.

Later versions of Christian ethics would highlight such concepts as duty and obligation; but Thomas (and medieval theologians in general) inherited Augustine's conception of happiness as the goal of human life. Aristotle, of course, did not anticipate anything like the face-to-face vision with God, which is central for Christian eschatology. True and lasting happiness, for Thomas, lies ultimately in participation in divine bliss. However, there is a happiness or beatitude that we can attain by our natural powers. Augustine, as well as the preponderance of the theological and especially the monastic tradition, not to mention the Cathars, did not value material well-being highly. While granting that earthly happiness is precarious, Thomas denies that it is impossible – health, wealth, and so on he regards as positive features of ordinary life. His sense of affinity with Aristotle allows him to entertain the possibility of natural happiness, transformed of course but certainly not diminished or negated by the demands of Christian ethics. Even material goods, if not indispensable, are not to be despised, and a certain fulfilment is achievable using our God-given natural powers.

Human acts (*ST* 1/2.6–17)

'Since we cannot come to happiness save through some activity, we have now to attend to human acts, so that we may learn which of them will open the way and which of them will block it' (*ST* 1/2.1 Prologue). While Aristotle's philosophical psychology and naturalistic ethics are constantly referred to, much of the material on which Thomas draws he takes from Nemesius (as he thinks: actually Gregory of Nyssa) and John of Damascus. Indeed, the latter's description of the operation of the human will provides the groundwork for the account that Thomas offers.

One point to remember throughout what becomes an extremely complicated analysis is that when Thomas thinks of the will, *voluntas*, he does not mean a power that one exercises freely and autonomously and even arbitrarily on things, but rather the susceptibility to be attracted to and drawn by the objective goodness of things as such: 'the most basic act of willing is the desiring of what is in itself desirable, namely goals or ends' (*ST* 1/2.8.1–2). The exercise of will is more like consenting to the good that one most deeply desires, rather than imposing oneself on something indifferent or recalcitrant.

The analysis is quite formidable. We are taken step by step through the phases of a fully human act: apprehending the good as the goal or end; wanting it; judging its attainability; resolving to achieve it; deliberating; approving and promoting the process of accomplishing the desired end; the practical judgement that selects which course of action to take; the choice; and the execution of the act. Readers familiar with analytic philosophy might want to translate Thomas's account into an analysis of the concepts which we use without thinking whenever we intend and choose and so on. He is not constructing a theory, let alone engaging in metaphysical speculation. To the contrary, he clearly thinks he is only describing what happens when we perform a moral act.

Certain actions are inherently or inevitably wrong, Thomas thought, whatever the agent's intentions, the circumstances, and the consequences. For Christians, many think, including good Christians, it does not ultimately matter what one does, what matters is one's intentions. One way in which we differ from the Greek world is that we place more emphasis on intention than on act. Thomas belongs to Aristotle's world. More specifically, though he does not name him in this connection, Thomas must have been well aware of Peter Abelard's moral treatise *Know Thyself* (composed before 1140), in which morality is held to consist in intention alone: what we do, the actions that we perform, apart from our intentions, are entirely neutral. Ultimately, if you have the right intention, it does not matter whether you fulfil it by doing anything, or not. Thomas could not be more opposed to any such notion. Of course our motives matter, but for him a bad intention is enough to vitiate an action that considered in itself is good in kind, while no intention, however noble, that can make an action evil in kind is a good one, under any circumstances or with whatever foreseeable beneficial results. It would be easy to compose a list of actions that Thomas regarded as intrinsically evil: theft, adultery, lying, and the killing of the innocent. The central defining feature of an action – what makes it the kind of action it is – is the *objectum*, its object or objective – namely, what the person actually *does*.

Emotions (*ST* 1/2.22–48)

What we do as moral agents is often affected by emotion. Often, the effects of emotion or passion have been regarded largely, if not exclusively, as disorderly and 'sinful'. The 'passions of the soul' (*passiones animae*) to which Thomas devotes a good deal of attention – love, hatred, concupiscence, pleasure, pain and sorrow, hope and despair, fear and anger – only partly equate with what we think of as emotions today. While of course we feel pain, we don't think of pain as an emotion, and so on. Moreover, so much has happened, culturally, since the 13th century, that Thomas's account of the emotions, very interesting as it is, remains rather thin and schematic, wanting in complexity, in the light of explorations by (say) Shakespeare, Freud, and many modern novelists.

The 'passions' with which Thomas is concerned always involve some bodily change: a man goes red with rage or pale with fear, his pulse quickens with desire, his muscles tense with hate, and so on. 'Passion, strictly so called, cannot be experienced by the soul except in the sense that the whole person, the matter-soul composite, undergoes it' (*ST* 1/2.22.1). 'The bodily change may be for the better or for the worse', Thomas immediately says: 'it is in the latter case that the term *passion* is used more properly – sorrow is more naturally called a passion than is joy'. Feeling is the basic animal response to the stimulus of the environment: affective responses by which we are attracted to the good, aggressive reactions to obstacles, and so on. Emotions have to be integrated with the dispositions of reason and will if we are to live a good life. While well aware of the dark side of some reactions, Thomas's account is nevertheless predominantly positive, with little sign of the suspicion that a committed ascetic might have been expected to show. To the contrary, this respect for natural physiological reactions to items in the world around us, including our fellow human beings, is only an implication of Thomas's conception of human beings as animated bodies, embodied souls. It is another indication of his rejection of Catharist hostility to material reality.

Virtue (*ST* 1/2.49–70)

Thomas distinguished between automatic reactions on the battlefield, which were the result of training, and acts of valour, which were rooted in a man's character. Sometimes we speak of someone acting 'out of character'; at other times, someone just acts as we should expect. By this point in the *Summa*, Thomas was surely hoping to get his readers – if they were young Dominican friars – to reflect on the practices of virtue, contemplation, asceticism, and so on, which constituted their way of life.

The English word 'habit' means a good deal less than Thomas's word 'habitus', or, lying behind it, Aristotle's 'hexis'. As Thomas notes (*ST* 1/2.49.1), the words, in Greek as well as in Latin, are rooted in some kind of 'having': isolated acts of generosity or whatever, are one thing; what Thomas and Aristotle have in mind are stable dispositions which a person acquires over the years, enabling him or her readily to act in this or that way. Discipline and self-control strengthen one to resist being misled by disorderly emotions, but they are not virtues (*ST* 1/2.58.3). For Thomas, there is a difference between a disciplined man and a virtuous one.

It seems unlikely that Thomas was explaining anything that his students did not know. They may not have been aware that what the philosophers of antiquity aimed at (Plato and the Stoics, as well as Aristotle) was exactly what the monastic and academic institutions of his day provided. The 'schools' of learning that were gradually becoming the universities were all collegial, in the sense that everyone shared in community life, eating at the common table, sleeping in dormitories, and so on; while those who were also vowed members of one or other institution of the Christian religion were practising life-long 'conversion of morals', in the old Benedictine phrase. People lived collectively and in public, to a much greater extent that we do in the West today.

Before considering the specifically Christian virtues of faith, hope, and charity, Thomas embarked on an exhaustive description of virtue (and vice) in general. It is as if he wanted to remind his students that they were human beings, endowed with reason and free will, as well as divinely called and inspired, and so perhaps inclined (as pious people sometimes are) to superstitious beliefs and indifference to intellectual challenge. In these considerations Thomas builds up what might be called a Christian humanism.

The main school of theological thought at the time held that the only true virtues were the ones that God works in us without us. This radically anti-Pelagian view obviously sought to highlight the indispensability of divine grace in any moral or spiritual endeavour. The School of Poitiers, on the other hand, inheriting this from Peter Abelard, was more reserved: Thomas comes down on their side (e.g. at 55.4 and again at 63.2). The divine or 'deiform' virtues of faith, hope, and charity come about in us without our initiative (they are 'infused', in the jargon) though not without our consent:

> for there is a happiness, a beatitude, surpassing our nature, which we can attain only by the power of God, by a kind of participation of the Godhead, as Scripture says, 2 Peter 1:4, 'by Christ we are made partakers of the divine nature'. This beatitude goes beyond the reach of human nature; the inborn resources by which we are able to act well according to our capacity are not adequate to directing us to this. Rather, to be called to this supernatural bliss we must needs be

divinely endowed with additional sources of activity – the theological virtues, so called because God is their object, inasmuch as they direct us rightly to him, and because they are infused in us by God alone; and because they are made known to us by divine revelation contained in sacred Scripture.

People can acquire many of the moral virtues, Thomas contends, by performing good acts that are directed to ends that do not exceed our natural powers. These acts are performed without the effects on the agent of the divine gift of charity. When people perform much the same acts but in awareness of the last end, then these acts count as virtuous, truly and perfectly. At this level, these moral virtues are imbued by charity.

> Only the infused virtues are perfect, and deserve to be called virtues simply: since they direct man well to the ultimate end. But the other virtues, those, namely, that are acquired, are virtues in a restricted sense: for they direct man well in respect of the last end in some particular genus of action, but not in respect of the last end simply.

Thus Thomas makes room for people who have moral virtues, which are not permeated by the divine gifts of faith, hope, and charity – 'virtues in a restricted sense', yet not completely empty, as many of his colleagues and predecessors (including Augustine) seemed to say. After all, 'Reason and will relate us naturally to God as beginning and end of our nature, but not to him as the object of a happiness out of proportion to our nature' (*ST* 1/2.62.1).

Just as real knowledge of God's existence and nature can be – has been – achieved by natural reason, while knowledge of God as Trinity depends entirely on divine revelation, so, as we should expect, for Thomas, though a truly virtuous life requires the supplement of the divinely given virtue of charity, there are humanly achievable virtues which are not null and void.

Sin

The starting point for this lengthy consideration of sin and its kinds, degrees, and effects (*ST* 1/2.71–89) is the attractive thesis that doing wrong, committing this or that sin, is a matter of going against reason, which is the same thing as going against human nature. 'Vice goes against human nature by going against reason' (*ST* 1/2.71.1). However, while obviously everything that Thomas says is affected one way or another by historical context, what he has to say about sin is heavily dominated by the doctrine of original sin. The problem is that Thomas's explanation of the doctrine depends on a biology – the will of Adam carried on through the male active partner in procreation from generation to generation, excepting only the one who was born without a human father – now unbelievable.

Parts of the discussion may perhaps be salvaged. Thomas distinguishes between venial and mortal sin: these are not species of the same genus, one might commit umpteen venial sins but that would not add up even to one mortal sin. Venial sins, as the word suggests (*venia* = forgiveness, related to *venus* = love), are no doubt regrettable, and damaging if they become habitual, but they do not deprive the sinner of God's grace and favour. Mortal sin (*mors* = death), Thomas believes, consists in a deliberate turning away from God as last end by seeking satisfaction in something created. This ensures eternal damnation unless adequately repented. On the other hand, to break with God in this way requires clear knowledge of the sinfulness of what one is doing and full consent. While Thomas of course believes in the possibility, and no doubt the likelihood, of our committing mortal sin, one might wonder how easy it would be for a person to reject God deliberately, fully knowing what he or she was doing – given Thomas's doctrine of God.

Even in connection with original sin, at least one thesis is salvageable. In the state of Adam before the Fall, which Thomas regards as historical, he distinguishes 'pure nature' from the supernatural gifts which perfected it. When Adam fell (not much reference to Eve!), these supernatural gifts were lost, by which human beings would have been drawn to their supernatural end, enabling us to keep our natural powers in submission to reason. On this view, then, their natural powers are left to human reason, will, and the passions. They constitute the human nature, which, as Thomas supposes, stands in need of healing and reordering by the grace of Christ – but they are not worthless, even in our fallen state we are not deprived of our natural powers.

Law

Immediately after this consideration of sin, Thomas turns to consider law (*ST* 1/2.90–114). That might suggest that he takes it that we have laws because we are prone to doing wrong – not an unfamiliar view in Christian ethics. However, apart altogether from our propensity to do evil, which certainly requires laws, punishments, and so on, it belongs to our nature as rational and social animals, so Thomas holds, that we shape aspects of our life together in written or (more likely) unwritten laws. Law is an 'exterior principle' moving us to good, namely, God, who 'instructs us through law'. God's schooling us by law, that is to say, is not only – let alone mainly – to prevent our doing wrong and to punish us if we do; Thomas sees law in a positive light, as customs and conventions that articulate our natural desire to know truth and desire the good.

Given that by nature we are drawn to the good, as Thomas thinks, we have a 'natural law', which, in particular cases and circumstances, requires us to think what we should do. For Thomas, 'natural law' ethics is another attempt to find middle ground, this time between the doctrine that 'it's right because we judge it so' and 'it's right because God tells me so'. No doubt he would have found the idea that we human beings create whatever moral values there are unintelligible – but he certainly does not want to settle for the idea that we simply have to submit to divinely revealed ethical standards.

He devotes one question to natural law (*ST* 1/2.94), in the middle of nineteen (90–108), of which three deal with human law, eight with the Mosaic law, and three with the New Law of the Gospel.

Human beings are empowered to 'direct themselves to an end ... through free will, because they can take counsel and they can choose'. 'Granted that the world is ruled by divine providence', as Thomas assumes we believe, 'the whole community of the universe is governed by God's mind.' The kind of creature that we human beings are 'is subject to divine providence, inasmuch as it becomes a sharer in providence, providing for itself and for others'. Thomas redescribes this: 'there is in us a participating in the eternal reason, by our having a natural inclination to our due activity and end'.

Moreover, this is what the Psalmist means, in one of Thomas's favourite mantra-like texts: 'The light of thy countenance, Lord, is signed upon us' – 'as if the light of natural reason by which we discern what is good and what evil is nothing other than an impression of the divine light in us'. Thus it is clear, Thomas concludes, that 'natural law is nothing other than the sharing in the eternal law in the case of rational creatures'.

Some might be tempted to think that natural law is a superfluous idea; the eternal law surely suffices for the government of the human race. Thomas rejects this line of thought: it would work very well if natural law were something quite separate from eternal law, but that is just what he refuses to accept: natural law is 'participation in eternal law, in some sense'. He would not endorse the idea of a natural law ethics which is autonomous and independent of theological considerations.

Turning more specifically to ourselves, Thomas maintains that we all have 'some notion of the eternal law', and secondly we all have within us some bent, *inclinatio*, towards what is consonant with the eternal law (93.6). Citing Aristotle – 'we are adapted by nature to receive virtues' – Thomas insists that we have a natural inclination to virtue, which may indeed be 'spoilt by a vicious habit', just as our natural knowledge of good is 'darkened by the passions and habits of sin' (93.6). It may be noted, however, that 'sin never takes away the entire good of [human] nature' (*ST* 1/2.93.6).

The same point is repeated, this time explicitly referring to natural law: as regards the commonest principles of the natural law, recognized by everyone, the natural law 'can never be deleted from the human heart' (*ST* 1/2.94.6). We may be prevented from doing the right thing in this or that particular instance, for example by lust or some other passion. As regards the less commonly recognized principles (not that Thomas spells out what these are), he allows that they may indeed be 'deleted from the human heart', 'either by evil counsel or by perverse customs and corrupt habits'. Robbery is not counted as sin among some people; sins against nature are not always recognized as such. It is perfectly possible that legislators have passed wrongful enactments against secondary precepts of the natural law. Here, clearly, for Thomas, legislation may, at least in some instances, run against the requirements of natural justice.

When he considers the 'content', or the 'extent', of 'the order of the precepts of the natural law', he equates it with the 'order of the natural inclinations' (*ST* 1/2.94.2). These turn out to be, first, 'the tendency towards the good of the nature which we share with all other beings' – to preserve our lives; second, at the level of the life we share with other animals – 'nature has taught all animals to mate, to bring up their young, and suchlike'; and third, as rational animals, we have a natural inclination to know the truth about God and to live in community, which means that 'it is a matter of the natural law that we have an inclination, for instance, to avoid ignorance, not to offend those with whom one ought to live amicably, and other such related matters'.

As created in God's image, fallen and sinful as they are, human beings retain an innate capacity for ultimately enjoying the bliss of eschatological communion with God. The soul is *naturally* open to a face-to-face communion with God, which can only be granted *supernaturally*:

> In one way, beatific vision or knowledge is beyond the nature of the rational soul in the sense that the soul cannot reach it by its own power; but in another way it is in accordance with its nature, in the sense that by its very nature the soul has a capacity for it, being made in God's image.
>
> (*ST* 3.9.3 *ad* 3)

Theological virtues (*ST* 2/2.1–46)

In the second part of the Second Part, Thomas goes into detailed analysis of the theological virtues, faith, hope, and charity, and then the four cardinal virtues: prudence, temperance, fortitude, and justice, together with the corresponding sins. These lengthy and fascinating analyses are essentially a Christian revision of Aristotle's ethics, richly documented, and drawing on an immense range of philosophical as well as theological sources. Only a few of the more controversial theses can be highlighted here.

One of Thomas's proposals is that we should think of the specifically Christian form of love – charity – on the analogy of friendship: a friendship inaugurated and maintained by God's establishing a way of life in order to share with us the beatitude of Trinitarian life.

Thomas rejects the thesis, standard in his day, that charity on the human being's part simply *is* the Holy Spirit inhabiting the human being (*ST* 2/2.23.2) – if the divine love which is charity is in us only as the Holy Spirit that means that we ourselves are not charitable people, or ever actually acting charitably and lovingly. That is tantamount to saying that we are mere puppets. Thomas, characteristically, fears that this implies that charity would not be human but that the human being would merely be the locus of purely divine activity, as if divine love 'uses the Christian as its tool and instrument – like a vessel or pipe through which the stream of divine bounty should flow unceasingly to others'. Thinking to honour the excellence of charity, the thesis only diminishes charity, Thomas holds. Humans are moved by the Holy Spirit in such a way that we actually perform whatever act of love. This returns us to the central insight – human freedom does not rule out divine causality – rather, human and divine causality work together in such a way that God moves the human will to act so that it acts freely – see Wisdom 8:1, a favourite authority: God moves all things to their goals by endowing each with a form that inclines it to its goal.

Cardinal virtues (*ST* 2/2.47–170)

The four cardinal virtues predate Aristotle, Thomas's source: prudence, temperance, fortitude, and justice. With these 'hinge' virtues (Latin *cardo*), Thomas is in a position to catalogue and categorize four great clusters of virtues and their corresponding vices.

Thomas pays much attention to the virtue of *prudentia* – much more than our word 'prudence'. In the English language, at least, the word has the wrong connotations; sometimes a virtue, more often perceived as a vice, it means a habit of being canny and circumspect, determined above all to avoid risks and undesirable consequences of a decision. For Thomas, on the other hand,

prudence is a virtue of the utmost necessity for human life
(*ST* 1/2.57/5):

> A good life consists in good deeds. Now in order to do good deeds, it
> matters not only what people do, but also how they do it; namely,
> that they do it from right choice and not merely from impulse or
> passion. However, since choice is about things in reference to an
> end, rightness of choice requires two things: namely, a due end, and
> something suitably ordained to that due end.... For people to be
> rightly adapted to what fits their due end, however, they need a
> disposition in their reason, because counsel and choice, which are
> about things ordained to an end, are acts of reason. Consequently an
> intellectual virtue is needed in their reason, to perfect the reason,
> and make it well adjusted towards things ordained to the end; and
> this virtue is prudence.

Thus prudence is an indispensable virtue for leading a good life.
Thomas means 'good judgement', the skill of grasping the salient
features of a situation, relying on long experience of resourceful
and responsive decision making – we might say practical insight,
even common sense. It is nothing abstract or abstruse. Rather, it is
a familiar feature of many people's character.

By far the most space in the second part of the Second Part is
dedicated to the cardinal virtue of justice and its many allied and
satellite virtues and vices. The 6th-century Roman Emperor
Justinian's Code of Law, recovered in the 12th century, was a major
influence in shaping the social and political institutions of the
West, especially canon law. Though aware of the jurisprudence of
the day, Thomas evidently preferred to go back to earlier
philosophical authorities. He starts, anyway, from the definition of
right, *jus*, as 'a certain balance of equality, *aequalitas*, as its very
name shows, for in common speech things are said to be adjusted
when they match evenly' (*ST* 2/2.58.1). Though allusions are
interwoven to the biblical notion of righteousness (*justitia* in the

Vulgate), that is not the focus. The central theme is the lasting and constant will to render to each his due.

The discussion is divided into justice in society as a whole (*justitia generalis*), justice between private persons (*justitia commutiva*), and to individuals from the social or political group (*distributiva*).

The first concerns the common good, which Thomas sees no need to discuss at length.

Distributive justice (*ST* 2/2.61.1) is concerned with apportioning proportionately to each person his or her share from the common stock – thus tasks, benefits, penalties, and so on. It includes the proper and equitable distribution of the wealth of the community. For Thomas, private property is a reasonable way of caring for things so long as those things when used by their owners are used in accordance with the common good, such that nothing is ever so privately owned that the common good cannot direct its use. Consistent with a long tradition of Christian and Jewish values, what Thomas describes is not widely practised or even accepted and understood in neoliberal capitalism.

Commutative justice occupies most attention: justice between person and person in exchanges, buying and selling, loaning at interest, and so on. The discussion of restitution is typical: returning something to its proper owner and/or making reparation for a loss or injury inflicted, so restoring the balance, *aequalitas* (*ST* 2/2.62).

The sins against commutative justice make a graphic picture of the morals of the day (*ST* 2/2.64–78): murder, bodily injury, theft and robbery, verbal injury in courts of law, inflicted by the judge, the prosecution, the defendant, witnesses and the defending counsel; followed by reviling, backbiting, tale-bearing, derision, cursing, cheating, and usury.

'Religion' is the first virtue that Thomas considers under the heading of the cardinal virtue of justice (cf. *ST* 2–2.81), perhaps surprising to us today. It covers prayer, worship, sacrifice, offerings and first fruits, tithes, vows, oaths, and suchlike; and the related vices of superstition, idolatry, simony, and so on.

According to Thomas, it is 'a dictate of natural reason that human beings should do something to reverence God' – though what, exactly, is not determined by natural reason but is instituted by divine or human law (*ST* 2/2.81.2 *ad* 3). The practices which display the natural virtue of religion (as he considers it to be) come under justice as rendering what is due: in this case, the debt of worship which creatures owe to God as creator. He places the virtue of religion in the context of honouring one's parents, honouring the sovereign, and suchlike – different kinds of honouring, as he says; yet clearly, he thinks, with a family resemblance. Piety, for Thomas, is not private feelings of awe; worship is an expression of the public virtue of justice.

Thomas has to make sense of the practice of asking God for such things as good weather, better health, and the like, without implying that God's will might be subject to change in our favour. As so often he steers between two extremes. God cannot be affected, let alone manipulated, by any creature; while on the other hand, petitionary prayer, no doubt the commonest form, then as now, cannot be pointless. What happens is what God wills from all eternity; nevertheless our asking God to grant this or that favour is not a waste of time. Creatures do not ask God to change his mind whatever they may think they are doing. Petitionary prayer affects, not God, but those who pray. On Thomas's view, we pray in order to dispose ourselves so as to receive properly what God wills to give us. We pray, so to speak, to change, not God's will, but our own disposition. 'We do not pray in order to change the divine disposition, but that we may ask for that which God has arranged to be granted through our prayers.' What we have to remember, Thomas insists, is that what is disposed by divine providence is not only what effects will take place but also from what causes and in what order they come about – including human acts as causes. We do certain things not that we might change divine providence by what we do, but rather that by what we do we bring about certain effects according to the order disposed by God. In short, putting it neatly: we do not pray in order that we should change divine providence, rather we pray in order to bring about what God has determined would be fulfilled through our prayers. Thomas quotes Gregory the Great: 'we pray by asking that we might deserve to receive what almighty God decreed from all eternity to give us'. As the allusions to human actions as causes suggests, Thomas regards the relationship between petitionary prayer and God's unchangeable will as one more instance of the double agency, the relationship between secondary and primary causalities, which lies at the centre of his theology.

> Divine providence not only disposes what effects will take place, but also the manner in which they will take place, and which actions will cause them. Human acts are true causes and therefore humans must perform certain actions, not in order by their acts to change the divine disposition, but in order by their acts to fulfil certain effects in the manner determined by God. What is true of natural causes is true also of prayer, for we don't pray in order that we should change God's disposition of things; on the contrary we pray so as to bring about what God has decreed is to happen through prayers.

(*ST* 2–2.83.2)

For Thomas, that would be superstition, a magical attempt to manipulate God, which must have been extremely common in his day. For Thomas, on the contrary, we pray as a way of entering the order of things in which God has decided that certain events will happen as prayed-for effects. As Thomas keeps insisting, there is no conflict between divine freedom and our creaturely freedom – on the contrary, in his view, the more profoundly we exercise our freedom, the more God is at work in us. It scarcely needs saying that this is another insight that cries out for further discussion.

18. Thomas Aquinas in the Demidoff altarpiece by Carlo Crivelli

More copies of the second part of the Second Part survive than of the first, which suggests that early generations of students lacked interest in the admittedly quite demanding discussion of moral agency, and even of law and grace. Potted versions of the second part of the Second Part, as we noted, were soon in circulation: effectively reducing Thomas's lengthy analyses to something more like the checklists of vice that he wanted to replace.

What his students should have taken away, and what we might highlight today, is an account of the good life for human beings, including reflections on the ultimate end, action, intention and choice, virtue and character – in short, what philosophers have recently labelled 'virtue ethics'. In addition, in the exhaustive analysis of the divine and then the cardinal virtues, Thomas delineates in detail what it is like to conduct oneself as a moral agent, as a creature endowed with reason and free will. Finally, since faith and reason, grace and nature, should work in harmony, it is no surprise, indeed it is absolutely appropriate, that Thomas could not have supposed he was doing any more than illuminating and reinforcing reflectively the lives that his audience were already leading. He agreed with Aristotle: 'we are inquiring not in order to know what virtue is, but in order to become good, since otherwise our inquiry would have been of no use' (*Nicomachean Ethics* II.1). That does not mean that he did not from time to time suggest ways in which his students might reconsider what they were doing. If they were tempted to regard their moral and spiritual growth in terms of sporadic outbursts of heroic virtue or repression of vice – sins or good deeds that one might count – then Thomas was inviting them to think of the moral life more in the light of a vision of the good and in terms of achieving a certain stability of character. If they were inclined to regard themselves as 'channels of God's love', he wanted them to be charitable people. If they were fascinated, as they no doubt were, by the almost endless lists of virtues and vices under the heading of justice, then he was surely hoping that they understood that all this was grist to the theologian's mill – even if there was little reference to Scripture and even less to Christ. If they thought they could change God's will by concentrating hard as they prayed, or worse still by attempting to bargain with God, Thomas reminded them once again of the principle of double agency – there is no competition between divine and human causalities: 'What is true of natural causes is true also of prayer.'

Chapter 5
Summa Theologiae:
Third Part

The 'whole theological enterprise', which is the *Summa Theologiae*, reaches its 'consummation' as we turn to consider 'our Lord Jesus Christ' specifically as 'demonstrating in himself the way of truth by which we are able to reach by resurrection the beatitude of immortal life': 'the everlasting beatitude which consists in full enjoyment of God' (*ST* 3 Prologue).

Christological questions come much later in *ST* than Christian theologians nowadays would prefer. Obviously, Thomas could never have imagined that the *Summa* would be studied in isolation from biblical commentary, as has happened for centuries (and being repeated here!). Nor could he have envisaged students of Christian doctrine whose days were not shaped by regular worship, penitential practices, and so on. They regarded the liturgy as continuous meditation on, and even re-creation of, the Passion of Christ. Their daily lives were supposed to constitute an 'imitation of Christ'.

The Christology of the *Summa* opens with questions about 'the mystery of the Incarnation, in the sense that God has become man for our salvation'. A theologian, whose thought is so entirely focused on the prospect of face-to-face beatific communion with God, was never going to base his theology on the 'historical Jesus', as reconstructed by New Testament exegesis. Thomas rests his account on the beliefs of the ancient Church about the unity of divine and human natures in the person of Christ.

The Incarnate Word (*ST* 3.1–26)

There is little here that is distinctively Thomas's own thinking. On the contrary, he takes us step by step through the moves that are standard in classical Christology. The mystery of the Incarnation 'took place by God's uniting himself in a new way to the created, or, more precisely, by the created's being united to him' (cf. *ST* 3.1). It is not so much that God came down to earth, so to speak; but that the world and humanity were taken into a new relationship with God, in virtue of whose immanent activity they exist. In the creature who is the man Jesus Christ, the entire created order is united to God: Christ being not only head of the Church but also head of all human beings (cf. *ST* 3.8.1–3). In being united with the divine, moreover, the created nature was 'not destroyed but rather was preserved' – a favourite theme: creaturely nature saved, healed, and enhanced, not diminished or annihilated (as one might have feared), by union with the divine.

One of Thomas's favourite questions is whether – given that something has happened – how appropriate was it? Given that God has become incarnate, as Scripture teaches, the first question is whether it was 'appropriate' or 'fitting', *conveniens* (*ST* 3.1.1)? That the Son or Word of God has become incarnate may well seem strange, unanticipated, and even inappropriate – but since it has happened, evidently and undeniably, it falls to the theologian to deal with whatever unease the fact may occasion. For Thomas, the chief pleasure of theological argument lay in showing how becoming the ways of God's dealings with the world turn out to be – once what has happened is apprehended and reflected on in a contemplative spirit.

Four reasons might make the Incarnation seem inappropriate: the divine should not be united to flesh; God always remains infinitely distant from the created realm; the divine should not become entangled with evil; and God, who transcends the entire universe, should not be enclosed in a woman's womb. Obviously, these are exactly the sort of objections that would be felt by those – particularly the Cathars – who regarded physicality as radically evil.

For Thomas, however, it is most fitting to manifest the unseen things of God through things that are visible, for this is why the whole world has been created, as Paul says: 'The invisible things of God are there for the mind to see in the things that he has made' (Romans 1:20); more specifically, what has happened through the mystery of the Incarnation is that 'the goodness, wisdom, justice, and power or strength of God are made visible' (cf. *ST* 3.1.1), as John of Damascus says, the great theologian of the Eastern Church as Thomas thinks, placing himself, as he no doubt supposed, in the great tradition of the ancient Church. He goes on as follows:

> Whatever is appropriate to a thing is that which fits it according to the definition of its proper nature; as reasoning is appropriate to human beings because this is appropriate to them insofar as they are by nature rational; but the very nature of God is goodness, as Dionysius says, which means that whatever belongs to the meaning of the good is appropriate to God.

Again, then, at the key moment, Thomas appeals to Dionysius the Areopagite, in effect to a deeply Neoplatonic concept of God as the sovereign good – goodness with the connotations of self-diffusive bounty:

> Now the very idea of the good implies that it communicates itself to others, as Dionysius says. Therefore it fits with the idea of the supreme good that it communicates itself to the creature in the highest way. But, as Augustine says, this happens above all when [God] 'so joins created nature to himself that one person happens from the Word, soul and flesh. Thus it is manifest that it was appropriate that God be incarnate'.

In brief, given the fact of the Incarnation, it is what we should expect, in retrospect – if, that is to say, with Dionysius, Augustine, and John Damascene, we already have an understanding of God as the freely and bountifully self-communicating sovereign Good. The God whose existence and nature has already been worked out by the great philosophers of antiquity (up to a point) from the existence of the world, and whose nature has been further disclosed in the history of the people of the Covenant (as Thomas would add), turns out to be the God who has united the created to himself in a new way (*ST* 3.1.1). Now that this event has occurred, it becomes possible and indeed desirable for the Christian theologian to work out how it was prefigured, however fragmentarily and obscurely, in natural religion and in the history of ancient Israel.

It has often been asserted that for Thomas there would have been no Incarnation but for Adam's Fall, as the remedy for sin. However, it is only after considering the Incarnation as one more communication of divine goodness – beyond the gift of creation itself – that Thomas turns to consider the question whether the Incarnation was necessary to save sinful humanity from damnation (*ST* 3.1.2). Again he highlights the Incarnation as 'advancing human beings towards the Good', citing Augustine throughout, and culminating with the traditional patristic axiom: 'God became man so that man might become God.' Moreover, he refers to the 'total participation in divinity which is truly the beatitude of man and the goal of human life, granted us by Christ's humanity'. Only then does Thomas consider whether God would have become incarnate if the human race had not sinned (*ST* 3.1.3). He knows of conflicting views on this question. His teacher Albert the Great maintained that, even if Adam and Eve had not sinned, the Son of God would have become incarnate. On the other side, as Thomas must have known, his Franciscan colleague Bonaventure argued that our only source for knowledge about God's will is Scripture; and everywhere in Scripture the Incarnation is related to sin. Given that the perspective in which Thomas sees the event of the Incarnation is that of the Dionysian conception of God as the freely and graciously self-communicating sovereign Good, there is surely a certain tension in maintaining that, but for the Fall, there would have been no Incarnation, and that the reason for holding this view is that 'what comes in virtue of the sole will of God, beyond what is due to the creature, cannot become known to us except as delivered in Sacred Scripture, through which the divine will becomes known to us' (*ST* 3.1.3). The principle that nothing can be known of God's purposes apart from what is revealed in Scripture seems outflanked by the conviction that the event of the Incarnation is the greatest manifestation of God's goodness (*ST* 3.1.1).

The first 26 questions spell out what one might call the metaphysics of the Incarnation: how the divinity of the Son of God should be conceived as really and truly united with the human nature of Jesus Christ in such a way that neither the divine nor the creaturely encroach on one another (*ST* 3.1–26). It has to be admitted that not only 'beginners' are likely to feel somewhat bemused by the arguments with which the many mistaken possibilities are relentlessly excluded. One argument after another demonstrates Thomas at work – how the divine and the creaturely are united in the incarnate Son of God is something (a 'mystery' he would have said) which can be illuminated only by steadfastly rejecting proposals that privilege the divine over the human or the other way round. For Thomas, as for any medieval theologian, it is by refuting plausible opposing theories that the correct view is reached. The true view is the one that remains when the mutually conflicting views have been rejected: what we should think is, so to speak, what remains when what we should not think has been demonstrated. Though aware of the temptations conventionally ascribed to the Egyptian heresiarch Arius (d. 336), denying the full divinity of Christ, Thomas is on the whole more concerned to affirm Christ's true humanity. He even corrects his own earlier statement that Christ's knowledge was so perfect that he never needed to discover anything; now, with the help of Aristotle, Thomas realizes that Christ had acquired knowledge like everybody else (*ST* 3.9.4, the only occasion in *ST* where he refers to himself).

Our Lady (*ST* 3.27–30)

Unlike some modern Roman Catholic theologians, Thomas treated 'Mariology', not as an independent field of study, but entirely in the context of Christology, between the questions on the Incarnation and the questions on the life, Passion, and Resurrection of Christ (*ST* 3.38–59). Famously, while conceding that the practice in other traditions of celebrating the conception of the Blessed Virgin should be tolerated, Thomas saw no need to hold any doctrine of her 'immaculate conception' (*ST* 3.27.2). Mary (like John the Baptist) was sanctified in the womb: he saw no reason to say that she was conceived free of original sin, uniquely so, in view of her destiny as Mother of God. This doctrine, defined in 1854 as a dogma that Roman Catholics must believe, developed first in England; it was propounded by John Duns Scotus in Oxford and Paris, then by Franciscan theologians in general; and was widely accepted in the late 18th and early 19th centuries, though long resisted by Dominican friars out of loyalty to Thomas Aquinas.

The Passion and Resurrection of Christ (*ST* 3.46–59)

That the Christian faith 'glories especially in the cross of Christ' emerges in the questions on the Passion (*ST* 3.46–52). The first question – 'whether Christ had to suffer in order to redeem the human race' (*ST* 3.46.1) – is a meditation on New Testament texts, insisting that God was not compelled to save humankind this way and that Christ chose to die. Of course, God could have redeemed us otherwise (*ST* 3.46.2) but this way demonstrated how much God loves humankind, provides an example of obedience, and so on (*ST* 3.46.3). Nothing here departs significantly from what any other theologian of the time would have said.

There is one noteworthy move. Asking why Christ's death was by crucifixion – death on a cross – Thomas brings together several patristic motifs: the multiple symbolism of the cross as tree of life, as that on which Christ was lifted up, as the sign that embraces the whole world; with the wood of the cross anticipated by Noah's wooden ark, Moses' rod, and the Ark of the Covenant, and so on (*ST* 3.46.4) – rare evidence of the richly symbolic allegorical theology in which Thomas was immersed as a boy at Monte Cassino but which he usually suppresses. In retrospect, being crucified between two thieves was extremely significant – here Thomas quotes Chrysostom, Jerome, Leo, Hilary, Bede, Origen, and Augustine, in a tapestry of patristic allusions. Question 46 is concerned with what happened, but actually shows much more interest in looking for the significance of the event in cosmic-symbolic terms than in working out the facts (as we might now want to do).

According to Thomas, the man Jesus Christ was caught up in the beatific vision of God throughout his life and even as he died on the cross. He endured maximum physical pain and mental anguish, yet nevertheless continued to enjoy the beatific vision (*ST* 3.46.8; but see 3.9.2 and 3.10.1–4). Thomas cites John of Damascus, as always his principal authority in delicate doctrinal matters: Christ's divinity 'allowed his flesh to act and suffer whatever was appropriate'. The cry of dereliction (Matthew 27:46), Thomas will claim, means that God 'abandoned Christ in death inasmuch as he exposed him to the power of his persecutors' – 'he withdrew his protection, but maintained the union' (*ST* 3.50.2 *ad* 1). That is to say, the cry of dereliction is that of a holy man who, in his suffering, remains certain of the love of his Father. The psalm from which the cry comes needs to be read through to the end, when it will turn out that the psalmist foresees salvation in the midst of his affliction (Psalm 21 (22)).

Here, of course, Thomas is only repeating the traditional doctrine. It no doubt tests modern Christian sensibilities. It is one thing to read Psalm 21 through to the end: thus to put the cry of dereliction in a context which deprives it of the horror of believing

Christ to be abandoned by God. It is another matter to interpret the abandonment as meaning no more than that at last the protection against his enemies, which he had enjoyed so far, was now withdrawn, but the test for modern Christians remains. In traditional language, Jesus was simultaneously a *viator* and a *comprehensor*: walking the earth while having the vision that the

19. Thomas Aquinas in *The Crucifixion*, 1437, by Fra Angelico, San Marco, Florence

blessed have of God in heaven. For Thomas, the continuous union with God implied in the beatific vision is only an implication of the hypostatic union: if the divine nature and a human nature are to be united in the Incarnation then there can be no suspension or cessation of the divine nature's being what it is without breaking up the union altogether. Finally, for Thomas, as in the tradition, Jesus is of the same divine nature as the Father – Christ's union with the Father could not be dissolved; it is a logical issue: no person of the Trinity can exist deprived of relationship in communion with the other two.

The rest of Thomas's discussion offers the same kind of interest: time and again he summarizes the pre-modern view, thus providing a neat starting point for comparison and sometimes for challenge.

The Sacraments (*ST* 3.60–90)

Thomas moves straight from Christology to consider the sacraments. He saw no need to discuss the nature of the Church as such. Scattered throughout the *Summa*, there are the elements from which a theological account might be created. In a good phrase Thomas refers to the 'people of God' as 'the gathering of the faithful', *congregatio fidelium*. He has plenty to say about bishops and the hierarchical structure especially of liturgical assemblies, often quoting Dionysius the Areopagite. He was of course well aware of the existence of heresy, schism, and other forms of internal dissent within the Church: Catharist clergy and laity remained a problem throughout his career. However, it was not until the 15th century, with the division of Western Christendom at the Great Schism (1378), that the nature of the Church as such emerged as a topic for attention in systematic theology.

Thomas finds it natural to move from the mysteries of the Word incarnate to the sacraments of faith, precisely because 'they have their efficacy from the incarnate Word himself' (*ST* 3.60

Prologue). For Thomas, baptism and the eucharist are primarily Christological events. It soon emerges that the sacraments of the Church, and particularly baptism and the eucharist, have been instituted for two main purposes: 'to perfect human beings in what pertains to the worship of God according to the religion of the Christian life and secondly to counter the failures by sin' (e.g. *ST* 3.65.1). The priority should be noted: perfecting the worship that comes naturally to rational creatures is mentioned before counteracting the effects of sinfulness.

The word 'sacrament' was introduced into Christian language by the African church father Tertullian (c. 160–220). The first great exploration of the concept of sacrament as such was undertaken by Augustine (354–430), another African as it happens: a sacrament is an action that, over and above its own distinctive and characteristic form, evokes some further reality beyond itself.

One distinctive contention relates to Thomas's solution of the question much debated at the time (and since) as to whether sacraments are signs or causes – only symbols or actually agents of Christ's intervention in Christian lives. Some of his contemporaries claimed, so Thomas says, that the sacraments 'cause grace' in the sense that God takes advantage of the occasion, so to speak, to bestow his favour. The rite of baptism, for example, would be the occasion for God to work in the soul, but the rite itself would only place the recipient favourably in the appropriate situation. The immersion in the font would not itself effect any change in the person who is being baptized. The rite would be purely symbolic – as an abbot is given a staff, a bishop a ring, when they are installed in office: staffs and rings do not make them abbots or bishops. In contrast, Thomas argues, as he thinks with ancient patristic authority, that the sacraments do not only symbolize a radical change in a person's condition but also actually effect it. Of course it belongs to God alone to cause grace, to sanctify the individual, as he hastens to say; 'grace is nothing else than a certain shared similitude to the divine nature' – yet, he insists, 'the sacraments of the New Law are causes and signs at the same time' (*ST* 3.62.1) – 'he saved us by the washing of regeneration' (Titus 3.5). Thomas refuses to accept the choice between signs and causes. The rites bring about what they symbolize – sacraments effect what they signify. As sacramental events, baptism and the eucharist are not only moments when those present hope for a divine intervention to coincide with the rituals, as many at the time seem to have believed. Rather, for Thomas, the rituals accomplish what they also symbolize (cleansing in baptism, nourishing in the eucharist). In short, Thomas was rejecting just another version of the occasionalism which he repeatedly sought to exclude: immersion into the water at a baptism does not only symbolize rebirth; the bread and wine consecrated at the eucharist do not merely symbolize the body and blood of Christ, they really are. This is, in effect, another instance of the double agency, which was Thomas's favourite theme: God's agency is such that the human action is also really and truly efficacious.

Eucharist (*ST* 3.73–83)

The idea that the eucharistic bread and wine are transformed into the flesh and blood of Christ is already there in the Apologist Justin Martyr (c. 100–65). More relevantly for Thomas, however, there had been a ferocious controversy, centred in Paris, since the late 9th century, over the distinction between something being present *in figura* and *in veritate* – 'figuratively' or 'really and truly'. An anonymous treatise dated to about 1140, originating probably in Paris and perhaps by the Oxford theologian Robert Pullen (d. 1146), contains what reads like an innovation, referring to the eucharist: 'not a transformation of a quality but, if I may say so, a *transubstantio* [sic] or *transmutatio* of one substance into another'. By 1170, this word is widely used, as a noun as well as in verbal and adverbial forms. The word first appears in a conciliar text at the Fourth Lateran Council (1215), in the verbal form: 'by divine power bread and wine having been transubstantiated, *transsubstantiatis*, into the body and blood'.

Fifty years later, Thomas is familiar with three different understandings of what happens at the consecration of the bread and wine at the eucharist: the substances of the bread and wine *coexist* with the substances of Christ's body and blood; they are *annihilated*; and they are *converted* into the substances of Christ's body and blood. He argues that the third of these meanings is the only acceptable one. He wanted to secure the presence of Christ's body and blood in the consecrated bread and wine *secundum veritatem*, 'truly', not solely *secundum figuram* or *sicut in signo*, 'figuratively' or 'symbolically' (*ST* 3.75.1). Some have held the coexistence position, – Thomas dismisses this, without much argument, 'as heretical' (*ST* 3.75.2). Others held that the substances of the bread and wine are annihilated and replaced by those of Christ's body and blood: this view is 'false' – it rests on a mistakenly materialist notion of movement (*ST* 3.75.3). Citing the 4th-century bishops Eusebius of Emesa (as he thinks), Ambrose of Milan, and John Chrysostom, thus deliberately reaching back to early Christian authorities, he holds that this 'change', *conversio*, unlike all natural changes, is 'totally supernatural, effected by God's power alone', and may be called by a name proper to itself: 'transubstantiation' (*ST* 3.75.4).

However, the bread and wine after being consecrated and thus now being Christ's body and blood still look and taste like bread and wine. In the jargon of the day, the properties or 'accidents' of bread and wine remain (*ST* 3.75.5) – but without the bread and wine of which they previously were the properties, existing now as accidents with no subject in which to inhere (*ST* 3.77.1–2).

Substance and accidents is of course Aristotelian terminology; yet Thomas explicitly bases his theory on the first theorem of the Neoplatonist *Liber de Causis*: the first cause can suspend a second cause, and thus keep accidents in existence in the absence of the substance of which they were the accidents (*ST* 3.75.5). In short, for Thomas, this unique phenomenon can be located with a degree of intelligibility only in terms of the Neoplatonic ontology of creation. Like the doctrine of creation itself, this understanding of eucharistic consecration completely surpasses anything Aristotle could have understood.

On the face of it, this account of transubstantiation seems to collude with the sceptical metaphysical doctrine that the way that things appear is no guarantee as to how they really are. Such a radical denial of the common-sense realism that things are normally just as they seem does not only depart completely from anything that Aristotle could have conceived but seems to threaten the confidence that Thomas consistently shows in the reality of the world that we inhabit. The properties of bread and wine that persist after the eucharistic consecration Thomas does not conceive of as in any sense illusions: a first possibility Thomas considers (*ST* 3.77.11). He compares the conversion of bread and wine into Christ's body and blood with the creation of the world: 'in neither one nor the other is there any underlying subject' (*ST* 3.75.8). The word 'conversion' needs to be ruled out in creation, we cannot say 'non-being is converted into being'. True, on Thomas's account of what happens, the bread and wine in the eucharistic consecration are changed, 'converted' – into Christ's body and blood: Christ's body and blood are not (so to speak) created from nothing. 'The common order of nature prescribes that an accident should inhere in a subject'; but there are plenty of examples of 'a contrary arrangement to be quite in order because of some special privilege of grace' (*ST* 3.77.1). Thomas cites the resurrection of the dead, the giving of sight to the blind, and, on another level still, 'look how some people are granted special privileges beyond the ordinary law'. He has just quoted the case of the conception of Christ in the Virgin's womb 'without male seed'. In the context of this array of miraculous or otherwise privileged events, so Thomas thinks, there need be no alarm at the prospect of our having here, in the eucharistic consecration, for a special reason and in the order of grace, 'accidents without a subject'. To the contrary:

> Seeing that all effects depend more upon the first cause than on secondary causes, God, who is the first cause of both substance and accident, by using his infinite power, is able to conserve an accident in being, even when the substance which hitherto as its immediate cause was keeping it in existence has disappeared (ibid).

The properties of bread and wine that remain 'free-floating', so to speak, after the consecration, are accorded by God's power the status of subsisting in being, displaying the condition of that utter dependence on God which is Thomas's understanding of the doctrine of creation. If, as Josef Pieper suggested, the idea of creaturehood is the key by which 'the basic concepts of his vision of the world are determined', we may perhaps conclude that, paradoxically, Thomas's account of the miracle of the eucharistic consecration only underlines what he owes to the doctrine of creation.

It is perhaps quite fitting that the *Summa* comes to a head in these questions on the eucharist (*ST* 3.73–83). In comparison, the remaining six questions on the sacrament of penance seem, if not perfunctory, rather dutifully routine.

It was while celebrating Mass that Thomas had the experience that made him decide to stop writing. The daily eucharist would have been the centre of his students' lives. It seems likely that having instructed them to see the Incarnation as one more instance of divine bounty, emphasized the true humanity of Christ over against likely crypto-docetic tendencies, and presented the sacraments as acts of Christ, Thomas would have been content.

Of course, much that Thomas discusses in *ST* let alone elsewhere cannot be taken seriously today. For example, he considers what newborn infants would have been like if Adam and Eve had not sinned: would they have had their full bodily powers the moment they were born (*ST* 1.99.1)? Would they have been adults from birth? 'No Catholic will doubt that it could happen', Thomas assures us; 'but it is natural that on account of the very great humidity of the brain in infants the nerves, which are the mechanism of movement, are not fit for moving the limbs.' Some animals have the use of their limbs as soon as they are born (Thomas reports what he has read in Aristotle, not what he has seen in the fields) – they owe this to the dryness of their brains. Thomas goes on, even more bizarrely, to consider whether females would have been born but for the Fall (*ST* 1.99.2). Aristotle, after all, regards the female as a male manqué – but for once Aristotle's idea is completely ruled out by the Bible.

The chief argument Thomas has against the possibility of ordaining women as priests or bishops is that they are incapable of exercising or even signifying leadership in the natural order and thus equally incapable of doing so in the Church. How Thomas would have dealt with the many instances of women, as abbesses as well as queens, exercising leadership roles, we do not know: presumably he would have regarded them as honorary men.

Of course, there is much in a 13th-century text which we find completely unacceptable, or unintelligible, or so embedded in beliefs and customs of the time that we could not salvage anything of interest. On the other hand, a text composed by a great thinker in a very different intellectual environment from our own can, precisely because it is so alien or exotic, inform us of possibilities and open up perspectives in ways which allow us to become clearer and more secure about what we ourselves believe. Few readers are likely to engage in detailed reading of the *Summa Theologiae*, which would take years (as Thomas no doubt intended). But a summary of the salient features to which we have drawn attention in the last three chapters may offer a guide to the initiation into Thomas's version of holy teaching. Of course, he expected his readers to continue to study Scripture and to take part in discussion of the questions that arise. It is worth repeating, in concluding this highly selective reading, that we don't know how Thomas wanted his most famous book to be used.

Chapter 6
Aftermath: Thomism

Whatever Thomas intended, the *Summa Theologiae* has been the principal text in the history of the reception of his thought. The term 'Thomism', recorded in Chambers' *Cyclopaedia* (1728), according to the *Oxford English Dictionary*, is defined there by reference to Thomas's views on grace and predestination. More recently, in the journal *Mind* (1884), according to the same authority, 'the Thomist philosophy' is described as the 'authoritatively imposed sheet anchor of Catholic doctrine'. These do indeed pinpoint the two most significant phases in the history of the use of Thomas Aquinas's thought. The first was the fierce controversy between Jesuit and Dominican theologians over the relationship between divine grace and free will, stopped in 1733 by papal intervention. The second was the revival of Thomist philosophy, endorsed by Pope Leo XIII in 1879, with the intention of holding off the infiltration into Catholicism of post-Enlightenment philosophies. But two other phases in the reception history deserve attention: the suspicion initially of Thomas's fellow theologians, and especially of some Franciscans; and, secondly, much later, the theory of human rights developed largely out of his work.

Condemnation in 1277

Thomas did not leave behind any 'Thomists'. What were to be regarded as his distinctive positions were originally defined by his

20. Pope Leo XIII (1810–1903), under whose aegis the philosophy of
Thomas Aquinas was revived

adversaries. In 1277 – on 7 March, three years to the day that
Thomas died – the theology faculty at Paris condemned 219
propositions 'prejudicial to the faith', including perhaps as many as
16 plausibly attributable to Thomas. On 18 March 1277, 30
propositions in grammar, logic, and natural philosophy were

condemned by the theologians at Oxford, some of these actions certainly being directed against Thomas. The condemnation was at the instigation of Robert Kilwardby (d. 1279), archbishop of Canterbury, who had taught at Paris, making his reputation by commentaries on Aristotle's logic and ethics, before becoming a Dominican and moving to Oxford. For Kilwardby, Thomas's philosophical theory of the unicity of substantial form in human beings had near-heretical theological implications.

It was his critics who began the process of identifying Thomas's distinctive teachings. In 1282, the Franciscans forbade copies of the *Summa Theologiae* to be made for anyone except 'reasonably intelligent lectors'. In 1286, the Franciscan John Pecham (c. 1225–92), a long-standing adversary in the theology faculty at Paris, who had succeeded Kilwardby as archbishop of Canterbury, had Thomas's theory that a human being has only one substantial form declared heretical. Indeed, he had the Dominican Richard Knapwell (d. 1288) excommunicated for teaching that there is only one form in a human being, namely the rational soul. Interestingly, 25 years later, at the Council of Vienne in 1311–12, the Church declared that the rational soul is the one unique form of the human body, thus endorsing the doctrine which Kilwardby, Pecham, and many others regarded as virtually heretical.

The theory of the unicity of substantial form goes as follows. Adopting the Aristotelian thesis that the rational or intellectual soul is what makes the human body what it is, Thomas laid himself open to critics who feared the implications for Christ's body in the tomb. For them – the majority – human beings are made up of three substantial forms: vegetative, sensible, and intellectual. We are not rational all the way down, so to speak. In 1270, when Thomas debated the question before the theology faculty, he was in the minority, perhaps even on his own. Assuming that Christ really died (and there were ancient heresies about that!), and thus that his body was separated from his soul (in the jargon of the day), then, if the rational soul is the unique form of the body, it looked as if the body in the tomb was not the same as the body of the living Christ. On the other hand, if we were to allow for a *forma corporeitatis* in addition to the rationality-giving form, that remained the same, inhering in the body before and after death, that would ensure identity. Thomas dispensed with any such plurality of forms in a human being. The man Jesus Christ was really and truly dead, his soul being separated from his body; yet, since his dead body remained united to the person of the Son, so Thomas contended, there was no problem about its remaining the same body. Aristotle's hylomorphic anthropology dispensed with the multi-levelled conception the theologians thought they needed, paradoxically enough allowing Thomas to highlight the doctrine of the hypostatic union between the human and divine natures in Christ. Far from distorting a Christian doctrine, on this occasion at least resort to Aristotle's philosophy only enhanced the theology.

The question no doubt seems arcane: how many theologians today would even be interested in the status of Christ's body after his death? On the other hand, Thomas's thesis, in purely philosophical terms, updated no doubt, that we humans are rational all the way down, seems as controversial as ever.

Early modern Thomism

Much later, as reports of the effects of the Spanish colonization of South and Central America began to trickle back to Spain, a remarkable group of jurist-theologians at Salamanca began to work out what would become the modern theory of human rights, explicitly relying on Thomas Aquinas. The greatest was the Spanish Dominican Francisco de Vitoria (1483–1546): educated in Paris at Saint-Jacques, once Thomas's home, he was instrumental in substituting the *Summa* for Peter Lombard's *Sentences* when he returned home to teach at Salamanca. Of course the *Summa* was widely available by this time, but it may be noted that it took about 250 years for it to become the principal text in Roman Catholic colleges.

Vitoria discussed the morality of the conquest of the Indies. He was critical of the Spanish methods of colonization in America. He is sometimes remembered as the 'father of international law'. He set out the conditions of a just war and held that no war would be permissible if it brought serious evil to Christendom and the world at large. Above all, however, the discovery of the native peoples of the Americas, and the tendency of the good Spanish Catholic colonists to treat them as animals and even to exterminate them, compelled theologians like Vitoria to consider whether these creatures had souls, and from there to contend that they had rights to life and property. Obviously, since the question never arose in his day, there is no specific discussion in the *Summa*, but it was not difficult to draw on Thomas's views, particularly on the soul and on the virtue of justice, to set out the foundations of the modern doctrine of human rights.

Domingo de Soto (1494–1569), also a Dominican friar, was another of the major figures at Salamanca. He is best known in economic theory and in theological circles for his defence of the price differential in usury as compatible with a Thomist notion of 'just price'.

Better known than either Vitoria or Soto, Bartolomé de Las Casas (1484–1566), who emigrated as a young man to the Caribbean, where he witnessed the cruelties of the settlers against the indigenous people, became a powerful opponent of colonialism. In 1522, already a missionary priest, he joined the Dominicans. His *Destruccion des las Indias* (1552), condemning the cruelties of the colonists, is epoch-making. If Las Casas contributed less than his colleagues to the theoretical articulation of human rights, his book bears eloquent witness to the appalling situation to which they sought to respond theologically, always drawing on Thomas Aquinas.

Of course Dominicans and Thomists were not the only moralists at the time who were deeply disturbed by the news of what was happening. In 1510, teaching in Paris, many years before he returned to his native Scotland to teach at the University of

St Andrews, John Mair (c. 1467–1550) discussed moral and legal questions arising from the Spanish discovery of America, insisting that the indigenous peoples had property rights that should not be taken away, at least not without compensation.

Later still, in the 17th century, the university arts curriculum in Scotland, then one of the heartlands of strict Calvinism, was overwhelmingly Aristotelian and scholastic: Thomas Aquinas, Duns Scotus, and William Ockham appear in virtually every set of logic 'dictates' (student lecture notes). As recent scholarship has shown, Thomas Aquinas's account of justice and restitution greatly influenced Stair's *Institutions of the Law of Scotland*. First published in 1681, Stair is the foundation of modern Scots law. Created Viscount Stair in 1690, James Dalrymple (1619–95) is Scotland's greatest jurist. The complex interplay between restitution, fault, and three-party transactions may find a rationale within Thomas's scheme, which partly explains the idiosyncratic nature of Stair's account. Dalrymple was educated entirely at Glasgow University, where he taught philosophy until 1647 when he became a lawyer. The complex interaction in Stair's thinking of his Presbyterian religion, scholastic philosophy, and commitment to the idea of natural law deserves more discussion. There appeared in 1695 *A Vindication of the Divine Perfections, illustrating the Glory of God in them by Reason and Revelation, methodically digested into several meditations by a Person of Honour* – thought to be by Stair. Quite independently of the growing recognition within the Roman Church of Thomas's authority, his ideas, especially on the cardinal virtue of justice (as in *ST* 2-2.57–62), were valued, as Stair's work shows, outside strictly theological circles, in the philosophy of law, and well beyond sympathy with Catholicism.

De Auxiliis

The fiercest debate within Roman Catholic theology was over Thomas's views on grace and predestination. The Spanish Jesuit

Luis de Molina (1535–1600) sought to reconcile the absolute sovereignty of God and the liberty of the human will by introducing the notion of *scientia media*: a knowledge midway between God's knowledge of actually existent beings, past, present, and future, and God's knowledge of purely possible beings. This allowed for a knowledge of beings or states of being that would exist if certain conditions were fulfilled. Surveying the endless possibilities, each with its own outcome, God chooses for creation – and actually creates – that which corresponds most perfectly to God's inscrutable designs.

The Dominican Domingo Bàñez (1528–1604) attacked this account on the grounds that it compromised the divine sovereignty by an anthropocentric focus on the interaction of God and creatures that amounted to Pelagianism. God moves creatures to action, but always according to their natures – and so moves free creatures freely. In effect, Molina had misunderstood Thomas's doctrine of double agency. This seemed to Molina and his followers to evade the issue, with empty rhetoric that failed to allow human freedom any degree of real self-determination. In effect, according to Molinists, Bàñezian Thomists were little better than 'Calvinists', denying (as was supposed) that human response to divine grace could be real cooperation, let alone 'meritorious'.

This bitter dispute was referred to Rome in 1594. It was considered from 1598 to 1607 by the papal commission *de Auxiliis* – *auxilia* being the 'helps' supposedly afforded human nature by divine grace. No solution was reached. Pope Paul V (in office 1605–21), on the advice of Saint Francis de Sales (1567–1622), forbade the Jesuits calling the Dominicans Calvinists and the Dominicans calling the Jesuits Pelagians. It was only in 1733, however, that Pope Clement XII officially put a stop to the debate:

> We forbid these opposing schools either in writing, or speaking or disputation or on any other occasion to dare impose any theological

note or censure on the opposite school of thought or to attack their rivals in offensive or insulting language.

The controversy rumbled on for a further two centuries. Learned books abound, mostly in Latin, written in the late 19th and early 20th centuries, in which Dominican theologians carried on the work of Bàñez, arguing that while of course the human will cannot be determined to a free action by any secondary cause, which would indeed deprive us of freedom, it can be so determined by God's motion. This is what they called 'pre-motion'. Thomas never uses the word. To these followers, however, it seemed a reasonable development: the human being who chooses a particular good moves himself to this good, yet this movement from potency to act, from being able to do something to actually doing it, requires a first cause: we who act freely both move ourselves as secondary causes and are simultaneously moved by God as the first cause. God's pre-motion is 'physical', not just 'moral', in the sense of drawing the individual by love of the ultimate end; God's moving the person to act would also, more importantly, occur as first efficient cause. God works in every agent but in such a way that agents have their own proper activity. We should not be trying to explain human liberty at all; our focus should be on the generosity of God.

Leonine Thomism

By the early years of the 20th century, however, Thomas Aquinas as a theologian, treated as the source of controversial ideas about grace and predestination, was overshadowed by Thomas Aquinas the philosopher, called in to equip the Roman Catholic Church with the intellectual weaponry with which to resist the advance of modern thought. Unless and until we have a philosophically acceptable account of how we know anything to be true or false, we cannot say what we know about God.

The story of the outburst of theological activity in the first half of the 19th century, as Catholic theologians sought to rethink

Christianity in response to modern philosophy, is largely unfamiliar to English-language students. Georg Hermes (1775–1831), for example, very influential at the time, held the Cartesian view that our only certain knowledge was of ideas actually present in the mind, yet that, while the criterion of objective truth lies in our subjective beliefs, it is still possible to prove the existence of God by reason, and then to demonstrate the possibility of supernatural revelation. Anton Günther (1783–1863) held that the mysteries of the Trinity and the Incarnation could be demonstrated by rational argument; that there was no real gap between natural and revealed truth; and that the existence of God could be deduced from analysis of self-consciousness. Antonio Rosmini-Serbati (1797–1855) sought to finesse Enlightenment rationalism and what he (already) regarded as an over-Aristotelianizing Thomism, by maintaining that all human knowledge implies an immediate intuition of divine truth. Against such speculations, theologians such as the German Jesuit Joseph Kleutgen (1811–83) turned to pre-Cartesian philosophy, seeking to recreate Catholic theology as it supposedly was before the late-medieval developments, which gave rise, not only to the Reformation but (much more importantly, for Catholic theologians, at this stage) to philosophy as a methodologically sceptical discipline. The rise of modern Thomism is intelligible only as the Roman Catholic Church's rejection of attempts by distinguished Catholic theologians to rethink Christian doctrine in terms of post-Cartesian philosophy.

The only way to prevent Catholic theologians from succumbing to the rationalism and subjectivism of modernity was to train them in the tough-minded realism of Aristotelian metaphysics and epistemology as practised by Thomas Aquinas. Thomists argued, in their thousands, against the scepticism that characterized post-Cartesian theories of knowledge, that there is no problem about bridging some supposed gap between a person's consciousness and the outside world. On the contrary, cognitive activity occurs when the form of whatever it may be in the world is realized as the form of the thing in a person's mind. When some reality which is potentially intelligible becomes actually so, the mind, which is a potentiality for knowing, is actually exercised (as we saw in Chapter 3). Against idealists of one sort or another, there is no *tertium quid* between mind and world, such as impressions, sense data, or any other entity that would inevitably open up the possibility that knowledge is not of reality but only of intermediaries of some kind.

Pope Leo XIII himself, however, was not interested in epistemology. He wrote as follows to his fellow bishops:

> While, therefore, We hold that every word of wisdom, every useful thing by whomsoever discovered or planned, ought to be received with a willing and grateful mind, We exhort you, venerable brethren, in all earnestness to restore the golden wisdom of St. Thomas and to spread it far and wide for the defense and beauty of the Catholic faith, for the good of society, and for the advantage of all the sciences.

Leo sought the revival of 'Christian philosophy' – 'Thomist philosophy' – in the context of the ongoing political problems: 'False conclusions concerning divine and human things, which originated in the schools of philosophy, have now crept into all the orders of the State.' He would continue his project in the encyclical *Rerum Novarum* (1891), an immense exposition of Catholic teaching on modern social and political issues, the foundation of Catholic 'social doctrine'. Like the Spanish natural rights school, he looked mostly to the second part of the Second Part, to the questions on the virtue of justice.

Pope Pius X's condemnation of Modernism in 1907 diverted Thomism from social doctrine to epistemology. The Modernists were accused of reducing revelation to experience, Scripture to history, and doctrine to symbols – in short, they were inclined to subjectivism and relativism. The Thomistic fundamentals were not to be 'placed in the category of opinions capable of being debated one way or the other'. On the contrary, the Vatican published a list of 24 Thomistic theses to be affirmed, certainly by any Catholic seminary professor. These began with an affirmation of the divine being as pure act, in contrast to the admixture of potency in creatures. The *Code of Canon Law* (1917) required those in charge of religious and clerical formation to teach the 'principles of the Angelic Doctor and hold to them religiously'. Thomas's fate was to become the principal intellectual weapon against modernity.

Only five months after Pius X's death, his successor, Benedict XV, declared that there is room 'for divergent opinions' so long as they constitute no 'harm to faith or discipline' and are expressed 'with due moderation'. In turn, his successor, Pius XI, in 1923 reasserted that there must be no deviation from Thomas *in metaphysical principles*. These must be preserved intact, even while 'lovers of Thomas' were allowed to engage in 'honorable rivalry in a just and proper freedom which is the life-blood of studies'. Like Leo XIII, he emphasized Thomas's contributions 'in the science of morals, in sociology and law, by laying down sound principles of legal and social, commutative and distributive justice, and explaining the relations between justice and charity'. He noted particularly:

> those superb chapters in the second part of the *Summa Theologiae*
> on paternal or domestic government, the lawful power of the State
> or the nation, natural and international law, peace and war, justice
> and property, laws and the obedience they command, the duty of
> helping individual citizens in their need and cooperating with all to
> secure the prosperity of the State, both in the natural and the
> supernatural order.

What he wanted most was that:

> the teachings of Aquinas, more particularly his exposition of
> international law and the laws governing the mutual relations of

peoples, become more and more studied, for it contains the foundations of a genuine 'League of Nations'.

At this point, in the early 1920s, the Vatican was hoping to influence the new arrangements for securing international peace that emerged from the catastrophe of the Great War.

In the work of the French philosopher Jacques Maritain (1882–1973), the American Jesuit John Courtney Murray (1904–67), and many others, a substantial body of literature on these subjects exists, including social and political philosophy, the philosophy of education, history, and culture, much of which was inspired by study of Thomas.

Harnack

There were less favourable views. Adolf Harnack (1851–1930) was no doubt the greatest German church historian and theologian of his day. For him, as regards Thomas, the basic error resides in the underlying concept of God and of grace: 'There was no recognition of personality, neither of the personality of God, nor of man as a person.' Thomas's model is 'communications of things' (*dingliche Mitteilungen*), whereas what is wanted is person-to-person communion:

> the disclosure to the soul, that the holy God who rules heaven and earth is its Father, with whom it can, and may, live as a child in its father's house – that is grace, nay, that alone is grace, the trustful confidence in God, namely, which rests on the certainty that the separating guilt has been swept away.

Not even the mystics had a real sense of this. Like Augustine and Thomas Aquinas, they all, when they thought of God, looked 'not to the heart of God, but to an inscrutable Being' (*ein unergründliches Wesen*), 'who, as he has created the world out of nothing, so is also the productive source of inexhaustible forces that yield

knowledge and transformation of essence'. And when they thought
of themselves – these mystics – they did not think of 'the centre of
the human ego, the spirit, which is so free and so lofty that it
cannot be influenced by benefits that are objective, even though
they be the greatest perceptions and the most glorious investiture,
and at the same time is so feeble in itself that it can find support
only in another person'. Rather, in place of the personal fellowship
with God, which is grace, they construed grace as 'knowledge and
participation in the divine nature'. The more impersonal, objective
(*dinglich*), and external this grace becomes, the less surprising it is
that it at length becomes 'a magical means, which stirs to activity
the latent good agency of man, and sets in motion the standing
machine, that it may then do its work'.

Thomas has 'the Areopagitic Augustinian conception of God' –
God as 'the absolute substance'. Though he rejected the pantheism
of the 'Neoplatonic-Erigenistic mode of thought', there are
traces of the idea that creation is the actualization of the divine
ideas. Indeed, with his thesis that God necessarily conceived from
eternity the idea of the world, since this idea coincides with his
knowledge and also with his being (the doctrine of divine
simplicity), it appears that the pancosmistic conception of God is
not finally excluded, the 'pantheistic acosmism' is not quite
banished. We have perhaps said enough to indicate what there is in
what Thomas says to give some plausibility to Harnack's wild
caricature.

Philosophy of being?

In the last 20 years or so, there has been a remarkable flood of
scholarly work on Thomas Aquinas in English. A quick look
would soon reveal significant differences over how to read
Thomas. Some insist so strongly on reading Thomas as a
theologian that others fight back, insisting that he wrote a good
deal of great philosophy, easily extracted from his theology. For
some, Thomas remains an Aristotelian, others stress his debt to

21. *The Triumph of St Thomas Aquinas*, 1470, by Benozzo Gozzoli,
now in the Louvre

Dionysius the Areopagite and thus to a certain Neoplatonism. One key issue relates to how we are to understand Thomas as a philosopher of being.

Consider some remarks in the late Pope John Paul II's encyclical *Fides et ratio*. In connection with Thomas, we are directed to consider the realism that recognizes the objectivity of truth and produces not merely a philosophy of 'what seems to be' but a philosophy of 'what is' (not phenomenalism but realism, in the jargon). There needs to be investigation of being – *ipsum esse*. Yet, what is this 'philosophy of Being' which,

> within the perspective of the Christian metaphysical tradition,... is an active or dynamic philosophy which presents truth in its ontological, causal and communicative structures, retrieving its impetus and perennial impulse in the very fact that it is upheld by the act of 'being' and as a result it possesses a complete and general access to a solid universe of things and goes beyond every limit to arrive at Him in whom the consummation of all things is attained?

John Paul II refers us to an address he delivered in Rome in 1979, speaking in Italian:

> the philosophy of St Thomas is a philosophy of *being*, that is, of the *actus essendi* [actualization of Being], whose transcendental value paves the most direct way to rise to the knowledge of subsisting Being and pure Act, namely to God.

He goes on: 'we can even call this philosophy the philosophy of the proclamation of being, a chant in praise of what exists.' – which sounds even better in Italian: '*filosofia della proclamazione dell'essere, il canto in onore dell'esistente*'.

In short, the desiderated philosophy of being breaks out into a song of praise, this ontology culminates in doxology.

Consider such remarks as the following, quite representative of the kind of thing that Thomas often says (*ST* 1.4.1):

> The most perfect thing of all is *to be*, for in comparison with everything it is *actuality*. For nothing has actuality unless it exists: hence *to be* is the actuality of everything including of forms themselves. So [*to be*] is comparable with other things more as what is received to the thing receiving than vice versa. For when I say 'the being of a man' or 'of a horse' or of whatever, to be is regarded as something received like a form, not like something to which existing belongs.

This is a strange way of talking. Thomas goes on, in the next article, citing his Neoplatonic authority Dionysius, to contend that, since God is 'self-subsistent being itself', *ipsum esse per se subsistens*, God 'necessarily contains within Himself the full perfection of being' (*ST* 1.4.2). This leads him, again quoting Dionysius, evidently with some delight, to say this (*ST* 1.4.2):

> To be is more perfect than life as such . . . a living thing is more noble than something that only exists . . . though an existent does not include in itself being alive or intelligent, because what participates in being does not necessarily participate in every form of existing, yet being itself includes in itself life and intelligence, because none of the perfections of existing can be lacking to that which is being itself, *ipsum esse subsistens*.

In the next article, again quoting Dionysius, Thomas considers whether creatures may be said to resemble God. Since the Bible tells us so (Genesis 1,26 and 1 John 3,2), the answer is obviously yes. Thomas spells it out – 'all created things, so far as they are beings, are like God as first and universal principle of all being' (*ST* 1.4.3). He continues:

> As Dionysius says, when Scripture declares that nothing is like God, it does not mean to deny all likeness to Him. For, 'the same things

117

can be like and unlike to God: like, according as they imitate Him, as far as He, Who is not perfectly imitable, can be imitated; unlike according as they fall short of their cause,' not merely in intensity and remission, as that which is less white falls short of that which is more white; but because they are not in agreement, specifically or generically.

Of course, as we are warned: 'Likeness of creatures to God is affirmed . . . solely according to analogy, inasmuch as God is a being by essence whereas other things are beings by participation.'

There is always the following reminder:

> Although it may be admitted that creatures are in some sort like God, it must nowise be admitted that God is like creatures; because, as Dionysius says: 'A mutual likeness may be found between things of the same order, but not between a cause and that which is caused.' For, we say that a statue is like a man, but not conversely; so also a creature can be spoken of as in some sort like God; but not that God is like a creature.

Creatures most resemble God simply in *that they are*, and in *doing what it is their thing to do*, so to speak. In effect, Thomas seems to be recommending a contemplative attitude towards *things* if we are to know anything about what *God* is like. Expressions such as 'Being itself' sound odd. For Thomas, however, the world is a world of creatures – composed hierarchically of an immense variety of existents participating in the act of existing.

Thomas conceives the being of a thing on analogy with an activity, which that thing exercises. This quasi-activity he refers to as *esse* or *actus essendi*, 'to be' or 'act of being', often translated as 'existence'. What exerts this quasi-activity he refers to as *ens*, a being, an entity, a sort of present participle of the verb *esse*. Then, what this thing is he regularly refers to as *essentia*, a sort of abstract noun formed from yet another present participle of the same verb.

The notion of being – of what it means to be – is that being is intrinsically self-communicative and relational through action: 'every substance exists for the sake of its operation', as Thomas often says, in some form or another. This runs all through Thomas's thought. Being is not a state but an act, being is dynamic, it's energy, it's act – finite beings are relational because they depend on one another, they lack so much; but also because they have a certain innate drive to self-communication, to enrich others, so to speak.

This understanding of being as naturally self-communicating to others Thomas inherits from the Platonic tradition of the self-diffusiveness of the good. Existing, for Thomas, is not being 'just there', as if waiting passively, inertly, in neutral, to have significance granted or imposed, or to be contextualized. 'Action issues from existence' (*agere sequitur esse*): existing is actively participating, playing a role, in a community of hierarchically related beings. Beings naturally open out in self-communicating action to and on one another, in a whole variety of ways, receiving as well as donating, and thus sustaining a network of relations with all its interactions. Whatever counts as a substance, as existing in itself, naturally relates to others by its self-communicating action, by the difference it makes. Being related in some way to others is the nature of substance. In effect, every thing is in some way imaging God – once again, in Thomas, the Christian doctrine of creation is the more or less hidden key to his metaphysical considerations.

Further reading

For translations of Thomas Aquinas try http://www.home.duq.edu/~bonin/thomasbibliography.html.

The standard biography by James A. Weisheipl, *Friar Thomas d'Aquino: His Life, Thought and Work* (Doubleday, 1974, second edition 1983), has been overtaken by Jean-Pierre Torrell, *Saint Thomas Aquinas*, Vol. 1: *The Person and His Work*, translated by R. Royal (Catholic University of America Press, 1996). However, it is well worth consulting *Albert and Thomas: Selected Writings*, translated and edited by Simon Tugwell (Paulist Press, 1982), which contains a good short biography and also sets Thomas in relation to his principal teacher, Albert the Great.

For the setting, see *Later Medieval Philosophy (1150–1350)* by John Marenbon (Routledge, 1987), which describes the academic institutions as well as the major figures. *The Medieval Theologians* edited by G. R. Evans (Blackwell Publishing, 2001) introduces the period even more comprehensively.

For good general accounts of Thomas's thought, see *The Thought of Thomas Aquinas* by Brian Davies (Oxford University Press, 1992); *Thomas Aquinas: Theologian* by Thomas F. O'Meara (University of Notre Dame Press, 1997); and *Saint Thomas Aquinas*, Vol. 2: *Spiritual Master* by J. P. Torrell, translated by R. Royal (Catholic University of America Press, 2003).

Of the *Summa Theologiae* there are two translations: as *The Summa Theologica* in 22 volumes by the English Dominican Fathers, in fact Laurence Shapcote single handed, on his own as a missionary on the Rand (R& T Washbourne, 1911–25, the one on the web); and as *Summa Theologiae* Latin text and facing English translation, with introductions and notes, 60 volumes, edited by Thomas Gilby and T. C. O'Brien (Eyre & Spottiswoode, 1964–73; currently being reissued in paperback by Cambridge University Press).

The best entry point for new readers is *Summa Theologiae: A Concise Translation* by Timothy McDermott (Eyre & Spottiswoode, 1989; Methuen paperback, 1991), with excellent introductory essays scattered throughout, on which I have drawn. See also *Holy Teaching: Introducing the Summa Theologiae of St Thomas Aquinas* by Frederick Christian Bauerschmidt (Brazos Press, 2005): selected texts in translation interwoven with stimulating theological commentary.

Drawing on far more than the *Summa* there is an outstandingly good *Selected Writings* edited and translated with an introduction and notes, slanted towards philosophy, by Ralph McInerny (Penguin Classics, 1998).

In the recent wave of introductory essays the following should be noted, all concerned with Thomas as theologian: *Aquinas on Doctrine: A Critical Introduction* edited by Thomas Weinandy et al. (T&T Clark, 2004); *Aquinas on Scripture: An Introduction to His Biblical Commentaries* edited by Thomas Weinandy et al. (T&T Clark, 2005); and *The Theology of Thomas Aquinas* edited by Rik Van Nieuwenhove and Joseph Wawrykow (University of Notre Dame Press, 2005).

Thomas as philosopher is explored in *The Cambridge Companion to Aquinas* edited by Norman Kretzmann and Eleonore Stump (Cambridge University Press, 1993). The best single volume is *The Philosophy of Aquinas* by Robert Pasnau and Christopher Shields (Westview Press, 2004).

Some not so easily accessed papers should be mentioned: in 'Emanation in Historical Context: Aquinas and the Dominican Response to the Cathars' (in *Dionysius* XVII, December 1999: 95–128), John Inglis makes the case that Thomas's theology of the goodness of creation is a debate with the Catharist heresy; Mark Jordan's provocative paper 'The Alleged Aristotelianism of Thomas Aquinas' is reprinted in his collection *Rewritten Theology: Aquinas after His Readers* (Blackwell Publishing, 2006); Wayne J. Hankey's superb 'Aquinas and the Platonists' is in *The Platonic Tradition in the Middle Ages: A Doxographic Approach* edited by Stephen Gersh and Maarten J. F. M. Hoenen (De Gruyter, 2002); a theme beautifully developed by Fran O'Rourke, 'Aquinas and Platonism', in *Contemplating Aquinas: On the Varieties of Interpretation* edited by Fergus Kerr (SCM Press, 2003). Trying to make sense of Pope John Paul II's talk of Thomas's 'philosophy of being', I turned to some wonderful essays from 1952 onwards collected in William Norris Clarke, *Explorations in Metaphysics: Being-God-Person* (University of Notre Dame Press, 1994). For creation as the hidden element in Thomas's thought, see *The Silence of St Thomas* by Josef Pieper (St Augustine's Press, 1999).

For the most elaborate reconstruction of Thomas's proof for the existence of God, see Norman Kretzmann, *The Metaphysics of Theism: Aquinas's Natural Theology in Summa Contra Gentiles I* (Oxford University Press, 1997).

For the aftermath, see *A Short History of Thomism* (Catholic University of America Press, 2005) by R. Cessario; *From Unity to Pluralism: The Internal Evolution of Thomism* by Gerald McCool (Fordham University Press, 1992); and *The Thomist Tradition* by B. Shanley (Kluwer, 2002), dealing comprehensively with central topics in contemporary philosophy of religion from a Thomist point of view.

Among the many good recent books, see *Aquinas, Ethics, and Philosophy of Religion: Metaphysics and Practice* by Thomas Hibbs (Indiana University Press, 2007); *Thomist Realism and the Linguistic Turn: Towards a More Perfect Form of Existence* by John P. O'Callaghan (University of Notre Dame Press, 2003); *Dependent Rational Animals* by Alasdair MacIntyre (Open Court, 2001); *Aquinas: Moral, Political, and Legal Theory* by John Finnis (Oxford University Press, 1998); and Fran O'Rourke, *Pseudo-Dionysius and the Metaphysics of Aquinas* (University of Notre Dame Press, 2005).

Index

Thomas Aquinas

Expand your collection of
VERY SHORT INTRODUCTIONS